Annals of Oxford

John Cordy Jeaffreson

Contents

CHAPTER I. ELIZABETHAN SMILES. 7
CHAPTER II STUART SMILES. 14
CHAPTER III ROYAL PUMPS AND THETRICAL SCENERY.............................18
CHAPTER IV. OXFORD IN ARMS. 25
CHAPTER V. THE CAVALIERS IN OXFORD. 35
CHAPTER VI HENRIETTA MARIA'S TRIUPH AND OXFORD'S CAPITULATION....46
CHAPTER VII THE SAINTS TRIUMPHANT. 55
CHAPTER VII CROMWELLIAN OXFORD. 65
CHAPTER IX. ALMA MATER IN THE DAYS OF THE MERRY MONARCH. 80
CHAPTER X THE SHELDONIAN THEATRE. 90
CHAPTER XI GARDENS AND WALKS...102
CHAPTER XII OXFORD JOKES AND SAUSAGES. 111
CHAPTER XIII TERRÆ FILII. 125
CHAPTER XIV THE CONSTITUTION CLUB. 134
CHAPTER XV. NICHOLAS AMHUREST. 145
CHAPTER XVI. COMMEMORATIONS...158
CHAPTER XVII. OXFORD IN THE FUTURE. 173

ANNALS OF OXFORD

BY

John Cordy Jeaffreson

CHAPTER I.

ELIZABETHAN SMILES.

ONE seems to breathe a purer atmosphere on escaping from the Oxonians who covered the Prince Regent with fulsome adulation, and returning to the scholars of the sixteenth century, who rendered to Elizabeth the homage of enthusiastic loyalty on the occasion of her first visit to Oxford after her assumption of the crown. From Antony Wood, the historian of her reception by the children of Alma Mater, the reader gets no revelations of ludicrous obsequiousness and revolting sycophancy. The gownsmen, it is true, testified their reverence for the supreme governor of the land by remaining on their knees whilst her coach passed them on her way from the North Gate, called Bocardo, after the adjacent prison,—an attitude by no means declara-tory in Feudal England of the personal abasement which it implies in Modern England; but, though they observed this requirement of formal etiquette, they appear in all other particulars to have conducted themselves towards their sovereign like intelligent and self-respecting men. Wood speaks heartily of 'her sweet, affable, and noble carriage but not a word of her 'condescension' in deigning to eat meat and drink good wine. And the contrast between the tone of the Caroline antiquary and the Georgian committee of academic toadies is all the more remarkable and significant, because the former was no person to underrate the sacred qualities of loyalty, and lived in times when general usage sanctioned an extreme respectfulness to rank, that had fallen into total desuetude before the opening of the nineteenth century, and when the fashion of addressing princes in what Professor Huber calls 'flummery' still prevailed amongst courtiers.

Like her father's appearances in Oxford, Elizabeth's visits to the national seats of learning were made with political design and for the furtherance of public ends. In deciding to pay Oxford the same compliment which she had rendered Cambridge two years earlier, she was actuated by a desire to strengthen her party in the ecclesiastical order, and to give the rigid Puritans, on the one hand, and the Church Papists (as Wood, himself a Church Papist, designates them), on the other, an opportunity of learning from the lines of her resolute, though feminine, face, that the imperious temper of the Tudors was one of the characteristics which she had inherited through a despotic father from an overbearing ancestry, and that Henry the Eighth's daughter was no less strongly qualified to conquer opponents and assert the principles of personal government than the monarch who, after driving the Pope's emissaries from his dominions, had answered the papal menaces with derision.

It is credible that, on announcing her pleasure to pass a few days at Oxford to the Earl of Leicester (Chancellor of the University), to Secretary Cecil, and to the ladies of her Court, she observed in homely terms, with a saucy, wicked, significant smile playing over her thin lips as she spake,' I mean to let the scholars see that I am not in the humour to stand any nonsense;' for certain it is that her demeanour in the schools was calculated to produce that impression. President Humphrey of Magdalen received a lesson which he did not speedily forget, when, on allowing that Puritan divine to kiss her hand, she observed drily concerning his canonical vestments and the notorious reluctance with which he had assumed them, ' Dr. Humphrey, methinks that gown and habit becomes you very well; and I marvel that you are so strait-laced in this point,—but I come not now to chide.' Thus Puritanism received a frown from the haughty lady, who did not fail to seize appropriate opportunities for frowning with equal effect on the scholars who were known to abhor the Reformation, although they had prudently conformed to the new ordering of ecclesiastical affairs. A strangely threatening light passed from her eyes to every one of the group of doctors who pointed out the place where St. Frideswide's relics and the remains of Peter Martyr's wife had been interred together.

But though she gave her enemies stern looks that troubled their sleep during many subsequent nights, she overflowed with graciousness to the scholars whose homage had, or appeared to have, the recommendation of sincerity. To the boys, who from their knees hailed her with cries of ' Vivat Regina as she entered the town, she showed a right joyful countenance, and exclaimed repeatedly, ' Gra-tias ago, gratias ago.' Of the Latin ' and Greek verses, which the Oxonians had composed in laud of her beauty and queenly excellence, and had stuck upon the gates and walls of the colleges, there was scarce a single set which did not elicit from her lips a few words of special commendation. With not a little of courtly hypocrisy she professed herself inordinately delighted with the series of wearisome Latin orations to which she was compelled to listen, and with the several disputations in St. Mary's Church and the schools, of which she was the attentive auditor. At one of these tedious exercises in the University Church, Dr. Kennall, the Vice-Chancellor, exercising his moderator's privilege, would fain have cut off Dr. Thomas Whyte, of New College, one of the opponents, because his disputations were too large;' whereupon Her Highness,—saving the prosy speaker from the sting of an affront which, but for her kindly intervention, would have rendered him ever afterwards contemptible in the university,—proclaimed herself so abundantly gratified by the disputant's good sense and admirably delivered arguments, that she could not permit him to be deprived of liberty to finish his speech in his own way. In which matter, most of my readers will concur with me in thinking that Elizabeth showed herself a considerate gentlewoman.

Whilst thus overflowing with affability to those of the dons whom she had no political reasons for regarding with disfavour, she exhibited to the un-dergraduates the hearty kindliness of an elder sister bent on making a riotous bevy of younger brothers enjoy a period of festivity. Arresting the lads, as they marched before her with their caps in their hands, she gossiped with them about their homes, proved their quickness in capping verses, and, tickled into merriment by their frank answers to her reassuring speeches, laughingly told them that they were saucy boys, who needed much more whipping than they got from their tutors. More than one blue-eyed, chubby-cheeked little fellow, she patted with motherly fondness on the shoulder, and dismissed with a kiss and a ' tip' of money, equal in value to the ' half-a-suflran' which George Coriat, Bachelor of Arts of New College, received for his ' pains' in welcoming the Queen and her retinue to that learned house, with a Latin oration.

One of the many pleasant scenes that arose out of her genial and frolicsome intercourse with the younger students, occurred in her lodgings, whither, for her diversion during a few hours of indispostion, was brought little Peter Carew (a child of old Dean Carew's family), who addressed Her Majesty in a Latin speech, that concluded grandly with two Greek verses. Nothing which she heard from the magnates of the schools, in the presence of the Chancellor the Earl of Leicester, the Spanish Ambassador, Secretary Cecil, and all the great lords and ladies in her train, delighted her more than the classic eloquence of this minute toy-doctor, who spoke out before the courtiers in all the confidence of ingenuous and well-disciplined boyhood She was so pleased that she declared that the child should not be sent away until Mr. Secretary Cecil had heard him repeat the oration; and when the minister, In answer to the Queen's summons, had entered the royal presence to hear the speech, she put the little fellow in good nerve and heart by saying, ' I pray God, my fine boy, thou mayst say it so well as thou didst to me just before It is agreeable to know that the orator did not break down in the repetition of his performance, and that on being dismissed from the sovereign's presence he ran back to his tutor, elated almost to a phrensy of joy by the gracious words of the Queen and her counsellor.

This pretty incident of the royal visit occurred on the afternoon of Sunday (the day after her Majesty's arrival in Oxford); and on the evening of the same holy day, Elizabeth was entertained, as she had been two years before on a Sunday's evening at Cambridge, with a Latin play; but, instead of imitating the Cantabrigians, who put a profane drama on a stage erected in a consecrated building, the Oxonians gave their performance in Christ Church Hall, which was appropriately fitted up-for the occasion with a magnificently adorned scaffold, and a profusion of ' stately lights of wax variously wrought.'

On the evening of the following day, Elizabeth was present at another dramatic performance in Christ Church Hall, when she witnessed the presentation of the first part of Palamon and Arcyte the English play which Mr. Richard Edwards, a gentleman of the royal chapel, had written for the occasion. But the success of the evenings amusement was grievously diminished by the sudden falling of a part of the stage,—an accident which killed a scholar and two collegiate servants, and inflicted serious injuries on five other persons. Had the mishap occurred on the previous evening, the Sab-batarians would have regarded it as the result of divine displeasure at the profane misuse of the holy day. But happening on the evening of Monday, the unlucky incident elicited no fanatical animadversions; and though the disaster must have materially lessened the enjoyment of the spectators, the actors continued their performance amidst much applause, when the dead and wounded had been removed from the scene of the catastrophe.

The evening of the following Wednesday saw the performance of the second part of Mr. Edwards's play, when, to heighten the effect of a point in the theatrical representations, a highly successful imitation of the clamorous music of hounds running on the trail of a fox was made in the Great Quadrangle of Christ Church, so that it was distinctly audible to the spectators of 'Palamon and Arcyte;' whereupon the undergraduates, who were provided with seats in the windows of their Hall, assisted the representation by leaping from their benches and exclaiming, 'Now, now,—there, there,—he's caught, he's caught,'—the imaginations of the boys being so worked upon by the feigned music, that they believed it to proceed from a veritable fox-hunt ' Oh, excellent!' exclaimed the Queen, 'those boys in very truth are ready to leap out of the windows to follow the hounds.' The part of Lady Emilia in the play —acted, it is believed, by Peter Carew, whose delicate shape and beauty qualified him peculiarly to represent a feminine character — occasioned the house scarcely less satisfaction than the crying of the hounds. When Lady Emilia, after gathering flowers in her garden, sang the song which Mr. Edwards had composed for her, she drew down thunders of applause from the theatre, and won from the Queen the reward of enthusiastic praise and a bounty of eight angels. That evening Richard Edwards had the delicious excitement of a young author's first and complete triumph, and after drinking a cup of wine with his friends he retired to a bed, whereon he dreamt of all the grand services which he would render to the Muses, and all the fame that would come upon him in the after time. But the author's hopes were almost as short-lived as his joy. A few months more, and life's fever was at an end for him.

What need is there to commemorate all the speeches that were made and all the feasts that were eaten during the six gala days which Elizabeth spent in the university? All such things are to be found in the chronicles of Wood, who has preserved for us the very words of the Latin oration with which the Queen herself concluded the act in St. Mary's Church, and the valedictory words that she addressed to the chancellor and subordinate digni-taries of the schools, when they had conducted her to the outskirts of the forest of Shotover, about two miles from Oxford,—the point where the liberties of the university then terminated.

More than a quarter of a century had elapsed since her first visit to Oxford, when Elizabeth made her second stay of six days in the university,—coming over from Woodstock to Christ Church, with a splendid company of nobles, amongst whom were conspicuous the French ambassador, and her faithful councillor, William Cecil—no longer Mr. Secretary Cecil, but the aged Lord High Treasurer Burleigh, whose descendant, the Marquis of Salisbury, is the supreme chief of the university to which his illustrious ancestor came, in the vigour of middle age and the weariness of dedining years, in attendance on the sovereign whom he served with glorious efficiency from the commencement almost to the close of her memorable reign.

In almost every particular the ceremonies of the first, were repeated at the second, visit. Again the Queen—no longer a woman in the possession of un-impaired health, spirits, and personal beauty, but an over-dressed and battered lady, with wrinkles and paint grotesquely visible on her sunken cheeks, a sense of growing weakness in her limbs, and a weight of gnawing sorrow at her heart,—was re-ceived by the authorities of the schools and the town with gifts and speeches. Again, as on the occasion of her earlier appearance before Alma Mater, she walked in state from her lodgings to divine service in Christ Church Cathedral, under a canopy upheld by four doctors of divinity, and between two lines of surpliced students, who exclaimed 'Vivat Regina' to the sovereign who, at her second coming to Oxford, was on the eve of the last decade of her existence. Again she frowned on Puritanism, administering to Dr. John Reynolds a rebuke scarcely less severe though something more mannerly than the angry scolding which Elizabeth's successor gave him at the Hampton Court Conference. Again she displayed her erudition in speeches of Latin and Greek, and sate at feasts provided for her by her loyal collegians. Again she was the auditor of scholastic disputations in which learned men ingeniously, but unintentionally, demonstrated the difference between learning and wisdom.

But the second visit was a poor and spiritless affair in comparison with the first. The royal lady had made considerable advances in the art of frowning, but she had fallen off so woefully in the art of smiling, that her smiles caused nervous men to look at their shoes; and when she strove to win the hearts of little undergraduates by patting their shoulders, and kissing their smooth cheeks, the boys were scared rather than pleased, and wished that the old lady would leave them alone and keep her bony fingers to herself. But still she retained the faculty of performing graceful acta Whilst she was deli-vering a Latin oration in St Mary's Church, seeing that her old Lord Treasurer was standing on his gouty feet, ' she called in all haste for a stool for him; nor would she proceed in her speech till she saw him provided of one.'

The drollest affair at this second entertainment of Elizabeth was a disputation, in which the physicians debated, ' Whether that the air, or meat, or drink, did most change a man?' in which wordy contest, says Wood, ' a merry doctor of that faculty, named Richard Ratcliff, lately fellow of Merton College, but now principal of St Alban's Hall, going about to prove the negative, showed forth a big, large body, a great fat belly, a side waist—all, as he said, so changed by meat and drink, desiring to see any there so metamorphosed by the air. But it was concluded (by the moderator) in the affirmative, that the air had the greater power of change' Dr. Ratcliff was the Banting of his period ; but, appearing ere the times were ripe for his doctrines, he failed to make converts.

CHAPTER II

STUART SMILES.

THE domestic politics of England in the seventeenth century may be described as the fierce and universal struggle of religious parties, in which the prelatists of the Reformed Church and the sects to whom that Church was unacceptable contended with varying fortune for the power to silence and persecute their adversaries. Not that this bitter war was restricted to the period in which it was most productive of public feuds and private animosities. Originating in the errors of Elizabeth's ecclesiastical policy, which, through a desire for outward orderliness, aimed at terminating the agitations of religious revolution before the natural time for their abatement had arrived, it raged furiously throughout the greater part of her reign, and cannot even at the present date be regarded as altogether an affair of the past But the seventeenth century saw the most violent and disastrous results of the stubborn conflict between the connections of men who in suecessive generations fought for the national church, and the connections of religious politicians who contended for principles antagonistic to the Anglican Establishment.

It was a favourite saying with the Puritans of the Long Parliament and the Protectorate that the war, which abolished episcopacy, disestablished the cathedrals, and brought Charles the First to the scaffold, was the 'bishops' war,' — a struggle that originated in religious grievances and had for its object the overthrow of an ecclesiastical government. And though they indignantly repudiated the form of a statement which fixed upon the prelates the obloquy of having occasioned the rebellion, the episcopalians of the seventeenth century admitted the substantial justice of their adversaries' assertion when, by according to Charles the honours of Christian martyrdom, they avowed that the royal martyr had laid down his life *for* the Church in a conflict arising out of politico-religious disagreements.

Deeming it desirable to withdraw popular atten-tion from the true nature of the struggle, our most influential writers and teachers in the last century were accustomed to speak of Charles the First's downfall as the work of rebellious subjects who resented his unconstitutional action in secular affairs, and were incited to insurrection by his attempts to levy taxes without the authority of, Parliament. Partly through the influence of mischievous advisers, and partly through misconception respecting the nature and limits of his royal prerogatives, the sovereign, actuated by innocent and praiseworthy motives, had made some trivial encroachments on the rights of his subjects, who forthwith, clothing their revolutionary and abominable purposes with sanctimonious professions of righteousness and evangelical zeal, avenged their unsubstantial and merely nominal wrongs by destroying a king who at worst had been but little to blame, and laying their sacrilegious hands on the property of an inoffensive and zealous priesthood. It was thus that the writers of histories for use in schools threw a veil over the real character of the social disturbances which an almost obsolete school of politicians conceived it to be their duty to misrepresent. But in proportion as Englishmen of the present generation are enabled to free themselves from antiquated misconceptions, and drive from their fields of historical retrospect the obscuring mists of prejudice, they see that the civil war of Charles the First's England was the thing which the belligerents on either side knew it to be,—a politico-religious contest between the Established Church and its multifarious enemies.

Acting on the impression that it was the policy of the crown to exalt the national church, which the Reformation had placed beneath the authority of the secular arm, and to repress all religious associations which were likely to embarrass or weaken the eccle-siastical organization of which the sovereign, as the supreme secular power, was the chief governor, Elizabeth was alike stern to the non-conformists, who ventured upon any grounds to resist the rulers of her church, and benignant to the clergy who, whilst discharging discreetly their spiritual functions, offered no opposition to her will At every period of her reign, jealous for her authority over the clerical order, she was, as we have seen, alive to the importance of maintaining her influence in the universities which the Reformation, by rendering them the principal seminaries for ecclesiastical persons, had endowed with a social dignity and influence which they had never possessed in Catholic times.

It was a necessary consequence of the condition of religious affairs and ecclesiastical interests in the seventeenth century, that the successive English sovereigns of that age were especially desirous to control the national clergy, and for the accomplishment of their designs on the clerical order sought to conciliate the universities by blandishments or win them by coercion. In these respects the two first Stuarts followed in the steps of the last Tudor. No sooner had James the First learnt from personal observation the relative influence of the Puritans and orthodox churchmen, and satisfied himself that it would not be worth his while to humour the former at the risk of offending the latter, than he threw aside the thin disguise which had momentarily concealed his aversion to the precisians, and, declaring that he would be master of his subjects' souls as well as their bodies, bestirred himself to be pope no less than king of his own dominions. He had not the resoluteness or persistency of purpose to surrender the delights of indolence and the pleasures of sensual indulgence for the arduous duties and sentimental rewards of a sovereign indefatigably laborious in discharging the functions of personal government in Church and State; but though he was for the most part content with boasting about the kingly honour, whilst his bishops attended to the duties, of his royal supremacy, he never ceased to amuse himself by intriguing with bishops and meddling with ecclesiastical affairs.

In like manner his son and grandsons, who suc-ceeded him on the throne, busied themselves in spiritual matters, and for the accomplishment of their very different schemes for the religious welfare of their subjects honoured Oxford with a considerable amount of attention. Successively the champion and martyr of the Established Church, the first Charles established himself in the university during the crisis of his struggle with the Parliament. Charles the Second, who was a Catholic so far as an inordinately frivolous and sensual man can be said to belong to any church whatever, strengthened the associations of Oxford with his dynasty by repeatedly bringing to her cloisters his counsellors and boon companions, his queen and mistresses. And whilst he found in the pleasant gardens and collegiate chambers of Alma Mater congenial companions and scenes for Sybaritic indulgence, he made his residences at Oxford subservient to his political ends.

Unlike his more agreeable and profligate brother, James the Second was too conscientious to feign affection for a church which he detested, and too superstitious to dare to postpone the formal declaration of his attachment to Rome until he should find himself on his deathbed. Confident of his power to restore England to the Pope by coercing the clergy with threats and deprivations, and influencing them through the universities, the unteachable Stuart, who bartered three kingdoms for a mass, had forced a Roman Catholic dean on Christ Church, and en-couraged Obadiah Walker to fit up a chapel in University College for the performance of daily mass, when he was constrained to despatch to Oxford a troop of dragoons to overawe the Protestant students, who were constantly singing in the High Street the ballad that begins with

'Old Obidish
Sings Ave Maria!'

A year later three more troops of cavalry entered the University with drawn swords, to enforce submission to the despot's violent usurpations in the seat of learning whose divines were meetly punished for having preached the slavish doctrine of non-resistance in being goaded to resist the tyrant, against whom, as the Lord's Anointed, it had been declared by the Oxonian pulpiteers that no subject might lawfully raise his hand. But before James filled Oxford with soldiers,—sent thither to effect Dr. Hough's ejection from Magdalen College, and silence the seditious tongues of turbulent scholars,— he had himself ascertained the impotency of his royal presence to allay the irritations and remove the discontents, which his suicidal policy had occasioned in the city that, of all the cities under his sway, had seemed to him the one least likely to resent his unconstitutional excessea.

CHAPTER III

ROYAL PUMPS AND THETRICAL SCENERY.

IN Sir Isaac Wake's 'Rex Platonicus'—a copy of which closely-printed duodecimo product of scholastic pedantry is preserved in the library of the British Museum—the reader, who has enough learning and patience to arrive at the meaning of the author's fantastic Latin, may ascertain with what costly pomp the Oxonians received James the First in the August of 1605, when that Platonic King deigned to honour Oxford by smiling on her schools and colleges throughout four festive and sultry days.

Isaac Wake, whilom of Merton College and in his most prosperous days a diplomatic envoy from his Platonic Majesty to divers foreign courts, was the most eminent professor and practitioner of Latin talk in his university, when the first of our Scotch sovereigns appeared in Oxford, to show the Southerners how scholars spoke the classic tongues in parts lying north of the Tweed; and it devolved upon the courtly and fortunate Isaac, acting in the capacity of University Orator, to clothe in fitting terms the sentiments of loyalty and grateful devotion with which the academicians regarded the sublime and sacred personage, whom the official spouter was proud to glorify as 'totius Europae decus et ornamentum.'

Though this honour and ornament of all Europe had not attained to the fulness of the corporeal girth for which he was remarkable in his later years, he was already a gentleman by no means undistinguished by protuberance of paunch, and his native brogue was in a high state of musical perfection, when in his fortieth year he rode over from Woodstock to Alma Mater's ground, in the course of one of those splendid and sumptuous progresses by which he was accustomed to prove the loyalty and exhaust the finances of his rural aristocracy.

Accompainied by his queen, Anne of Dennark, regiae domus columen,' as the judicious orator termed her, and Henry Prince of Wales, orbis Bri-tannici spes et deliciae,' James entered the university on horseback, his companions and attendants constituting perhaps the most numerous and gorgeous cavalcade that had ever appeared in Oxford for a festal purpose. The sovereign was preceded by the Duke of Lennox bearing the sword of state; the steeds, which bore the royal travellers, 'tam sacro pondere superbientes,' caracoled and curvetted in graceful obedience to the discipline of the *mnanege*, described in his Grace of Newcastle's ' La Methode nouvelle de dresser les Chevaux;' and in the flood of splendid equestrians, who had place in the glittering throng of adroit riders and mettlesome animals, were present the Lady Arabella Stuart, the Countesses of Bedford, Suffolk, Nottingham, and Montgomery, sixteen earls, and a mob of barons and knights whose wealth and rank were not superior to their lineage and fashion.

Never had England possessed a sovereign more highly qualified to enjoy the usual incidents of an aca-demic festival than the king, who would have found his natural and appropriate place in society had fortune made him a village' dominie,' invested with authority to whip little boys for mistakes in grammar, and unfold to them in grandiloquent language the mysteries of the Latin Accidence. Never had the lucky Scot been more thoroughly convinced of his immeasurable superiority to the rest of human kind than when he explained to his guid queen and her lad the meaning of the vara apposeet Grake oration which Dr. Pevin delivered to his majesty from the little pew erected for the doctor's convenience at Quatervois. Even at this distance of time one can hear the pompous intonations of the Scotch Latin with which he declared his satisfaction with the erudite and scholasticsl effusion of Mr. Orator Wake. And to Oxford's credit it must be allowed that she did her best to tickle Solomon's self-love. She gave him presents and fair speeches ; she placed Christ Church at his service, whilst Magdalen was made a residence for his son; she entertained him with a grand musical service in her cathedral, to which he marched under a royal canopy, borne over his sacred head by four scarlet-robed doctors of divinity; she provided for his diversion a dramatic entertainment in Christ Church Hall, where the students of the house acted a comedy with 'great applause; she gave him a succession of banquets and formal disputations; and when Solomon, condescending to take part in the exercises of the schools, delivered himself of a Latin speech in St Mary's Church, he was 'sufficiently applauded by the scholars by clapping of hands and humming, which, though strange to him at first hearing,' says Wood, ' yet when he understood, upon inquiry, what that noise meant (which they told him signified applause), was very well content' From the inarticulate flattery of such' hummers as those who hummed James the First into good contentment with himself, came the familiar term of humbug' and the signification put upon 'to hum' when the expression means to ' impose upon by insincere praise.'

Sixteen years later, James the First was again entertained by the Oxonians with a dramatic per-formance, when Barton Holyday's miserable comedy, 'The Marriage of Arts—modified and improved, or at. least altered with a view to improving it, since its first unsuccessful presentation in 1617,—was acted before the King by a company of scholars, who, either through histrionic incompetence or untimely in- dulgence in wine, occasioned the sovereign such dissatisfaction, that he was twice upon the point of leaving the theatre before the conclusion of the play, and was with difficulty persuaded by his courtiers to retain his seat till the fall of the curtain. Whereupon one of the several wits, who used their pens to bring the drama and its actors into contempt, composed the epigram,

'At Christ Church Marriage done before the King,
Least that those mates should want an offering,
The Bang himself did offer, what, I pray ?
He offered twice or thrice to go away.

In the fifth year of his reign, Charles the First, accompanied by Henrietta Maria, still in the possession of her girlish delicacy of form and lineaments, and attended by a splendid company of nobles, paid Oxford a visit of a few hours, on which oc- casion their majesties were regaled with a sumptuous banquet in the college, where the Queen at a later and darker period of her career presided over the court of fair ladies and brave men, who assembled from almost every quarter of the kingdom at the university, which had become the head-quarters of the Royalists.

In 1636, whilst Henrietta Maria was yet in the hey-day of her beauty and the sunshine of royal prosperity, and little imagined what dark storms were about to break upon her husband's throne and family, Charles paid Oxford a longer and more ceremonious visit to celebrate the Laudian restoration of academic discipline, and speak in commendation of the recently-enacted Caroline statutes, of which mention has been made in a previous chapter.

All Oxford turned out to welcome the royal visitors, who were received by the chiefs of the university and town on the Woodstock Road, whence they were conducted through lines of vociferous gownsmen and populace, and buildings decorated with gay flags and streamers, and scaffolds dangerously burdened with spectators in their holiday clothes, to Christ Church, which house of royal foundation divided with St. John's, Chancellor Laud's College, the chief labours and honours of entertaining the courtly throng. No scholar or person of the town, with health and means to witness the spectacle, was absent from the hilarious and picturesque scene. Every window, and balcony, and roof along the line taken by the procession was crowded with beholders of every age; and amongst the tiny children who were tricked out in their gayest dresses, and taken to places where they could securely gaze at the pageant, was a three-years'-old boy, who shouted himself hoarse long before his eyes rested for a few seconds on the coach in which Charles Stuart, Henrietta Maria, Charles the Elector Palatine, and Prince Rupert, passed slowly down the rough-paved thoroughfare and under the arch of the great gate of Christ Church. This little fellow was no other than Antony Wood, who in due course became the historian of the university, of which his father was a member, and who did not fail to commemorate in his 'Annals' and autobiographic memoir the delight with which he watched the passage of the royal party from a garden which commanded a view of the line of route. ' The King, Queen, Prince Rupert, many of the nobility and others says the autobiographer,' came from Woodstock into Oxon, a little before which time he' (*i.e.* the writer) ' was conveyed in a servant's armes, with his father and mother, to the lodgings of Dr. Tho. Iies, canon of Christ Church, whence being conveyed to the mount in his garden looking into Fish Street, he saw the K. Qu. and the rest riding down the saide street into Ch. Ch. great Quadrangle.

This was the first time he ever saw the said K. and Queen, and the first time that he ever saw such a glorious Traine as that was, which he would often talk of when he was a man.'

The ceremonies and arrangements of this royal reception—in which Laud arrogated as far as possible to himself all the merit and glory of the entertainers' share in the proceedings—differed in some particulars from those of previous celebrations of the same kind.

To impress on the academic community that the presence of the sovereign was due to his influence, and to give éclat to his college which, notwithstanding his munificent benefactions to it, had no claim to the King's special notice, apart from the importance accruing to it from the primate's patronage, Laud contrived that St. John's, lying on the outskirts of the town, should play a part in the gala altogether disproportionate to its magnitude and ordinary influence. On entering the city the royal visitors made a stand at the gate of the favoured college, one of whose members delivered an oration to the King; and the greater part of one entire day was passed by the illustrious guests in the same house, where they were grandly entertained with music, a feast, and a dramatic performance.

On arriving at St. John's they 'saw the new building that the Chancellor had at his own charges lately erected. That done, the Chancellor,' says Wood, ' attended them up the library stairs, where, as soon as they began to ascend, certain musicians above entertained them with a short song fitted and timed to the ascending the stairs. In the library they were welcomed to the college with a short speech by one of the fellows called Abr. Wright. That being done, and dinner ready, they passed from that to the new library, lately built by our Chancellor; where the King, Queen, and Prince Elector dined at one table, standing across at the upper or north end, and Prince Rupert, with all the lords and ladies at a long table, reaching almost from one end to the other, at which all the gallantries and beauties of the kingdom seemed to meet. All other tables, to the number of thirteen besides the said two, were disposed in several chambers in the college, and had men and scholars appointed to attend them to theirs, and the content of all "I thank God (saith the

Chancellor) I had the happiness that all things were in verie good order, and that no man went out of the gates, courtier or other, but contented, which was a happiness quite beyond expectation." When the dinner was ended he attended the King and Queen, together with the nobles, into several withdrawing chambers, where they entertained themselves for the space of an hour. In the meantime he caused the windows of the Common Hall or Refectory to be shut, candles lighted and all things to be made ready for the play, which was then to begin, called " The Hospitall of Lovers," made for the most part (as 'tis said) by Mr. George Wild, fellow of St. John's College. When these things were fitted he gave notice to the King and Queen, and attended them into the hall, whither he had the happiness to bring them by a way prepared from the presence lodgings to the hall without the least disturbance. He had the hall kept so fresh and cool that there was not any one person when the King and Queen came into it. The princes, nobles, and ladies, entered the same way with the King, and then presently another door was opened below, to fill the hall with the better sort of company. All being settled the play was began and acted. The plot good and action. It was merry and without offence, and so gave a great deal of content, which I doubt cannot be said of any play acted in the play-houses belonging to the King and Duke, since 1660. In the middle of the play the Chancellor ordered a short banquet for the King and Queen, lords and ladies. And the college was at that time so well furnisht, as that they did not borrow any one actor from any college in the university.

In reference to the religious character of the relation in which Charles, as supreme governor of the Church, stood to the most ancient and powerful seminary of the Anglican clergy, the Primate Chan-mechanical arrangements of the stagae Besides being furnished with three or four openings on either side, through which the actors passed to or from the boards, the stage erected in Christ Church Hall was fitted with 'partitions much resembling the desks or studies in a library which moveable structures occupied the spaces between the passages for the ingress and egress of the actors, and constituted a series of side-scenes. ' The said partitions says Wood, ' they could draw in and out at their pleasure upon a sudden, and thrust out new in their places, according to the nature of the scene, whereon were represented churches, dwelling-houses, palaces, &c., which for its variety bred very great admiration. Over all was delicate painting, resembling the sky, clouds, &c. At the upper end a great fair sheet of two leaves that opened and shut without any visible help. Within which was set forth the emblems of the whole play in a very sumptuous manner. Therein was the perfect resemblance of the billows of the sea rolling, and an artificial island, with churches and houses waving up and down and floating, as also rocks, trees, and hills. Many other fine pieces of work and landscape did also appear at the sundry openings thereof, and a chair also seen to come gliding on the stage without any visible help. All these representations, being the first (as I have been . informed) that were used on the English stage, and therefore giving great content, I have been, there-fore, the more punctual in describing them, to the end that posterity might know that what is now seen in the play-houses at London belonging to his Majesty and the Duke of York is originally due to the invention of Oxford scholars.'

'Passions Calmed' was acted before the royal party on Monday evening, when the illustrious spectators were so delighted with the new contrivances for scenic effect that they again visited the Christ Church Theatre, on the evening of the following day, after they had witnessed the performance of ' The Hospitall of Lovers' in the hall of St John's College. But on the occasion of their second visit, ' The Royal Slave,' a comedy written by Mr. William Cartwright of Christ Church, was substituted for the tame and lifeless piece of 'Passions Calmed—a change which was all the more acceptable to the Queen and her ladies, as the scholars were provided with another series of sliding scenes for its proper representation. 'Within the shuts,' observes An-tony Wood, describing the second performance with agreeable enthusiasm and simplicity, ' were seen a curious temple and the sun shining over it, delightful forests also, and other prospects. Within the great shuts mentioned before were seen villages, and men visibly appearing in them, going up and down, here and there, about their business. The interludes thereof were represented with as much variety of scenes and motions as the great wit of Inigo Jones (well skilled in setting out a Court Masque to the best advantage) could extend unto. It was very well pen'd and acted, and the strangeness of the Persian habits gave great content All men came forth very well contented, and full of applause of what they had seen and heard. "It was the day of St. Felix" (as the Chancellor observed) "and all things went happy"

The dramatic tastes of Henrietta Maria were so highly gratified by the new scenery and dresses used in the performance of ' The Royal Slave that some six weeks after her visit to the university she requested Archbishop Laud to procure from Christ Church a loan of the attire and scenic apparatus, in order that her own players might act the same drama before her at Hampton Court,— a request that of course was speedily followed by the transportation of the 'cloaths and perspectives of the stage from Oxford to the royal palace at Hampton.

CHAPTER IV.

OXFORD IN ARMS.

THE Oxonian of the present day may do worse things for himself in the way of intellectual amusement and imaginative recreation, than wander through the courts and gardens of his university, endeavouring to realize the scenes and excitements which made up the life of Oxford during the period to which Bishop Fell recurred in the last year of Charles the Second's reign, when he remarked in ' The Life of Richard Allestree, D.D.' When the war broke out, he '(Allestree) had the benefit of being, instead of one, in several universities ; Oxford was then an epitome of the whole nation, and all the business of it; there was here the court, the garrison, the flower of the nobility and gentry, lawyers and divines of all England. And times of action have somewhat peculiar in them to ferment and invigorate the mind, which is enervated by the softness of peace.

For several generations historical cant has so consistently and loudly commended the universities for their loyalty in siding with Charles the First during the civil troubles of his reign, that the ordinary reader requires to be reminded that it was the sovereign who espoused the quarrel of the universities, and lost his crown and life by contending against the majority of his people, whose allegiance he would never have forfeited, and might at almost any period of the war have regained, had it not been for his devotion to episcopacy, and for the embarrassments arising from his connection with the episcopal clergy. In the fight between the supporters and adversaries of the Established Church, Oxford and Cambridge—the schools of the episcopal clergy and the nurseries of episcopal sentiment—were of course on the side of the ecclesiastical institutions, from which Charles never withdrew his attachment though circumstances compelled him to consent to measures greatly prejudicial to them. In going cor-dially with the crown in the civil struggle the royalist ecclesiastics merely strove for the triumph of their own cause; and it was less to their own welfare than to the misfortune of the country that they found an ally in the sovereign who ruined him-self in their behalf.

But though the gownsmen of Oxford and Cam-bridge for the most part admired Laud and abhorred the Parliament, it may not be imagined that the academic populations were altogether without a leaven of puritanical sympathy. Whilst Cambridge contained a considerable minority of scholars, to whom the Earl of Manchester's measures for the government of the university appeared no less defensible and salutary, than they seemed barbarous and hurtful to the authors of the ' Querela Cantabrigiensis Oxford numbered amongst her teachers and learners many academicians who detested the Laudian church-movement and had no affection for prelacy. The peculiar abodes of these Oxonian Puritans were New Inn Hall, which, under the government of Principal Rogers, furnished for a consi-derable period forty new names annually to Alma Mater's matriculation-book, and Magdalen Hall, which, under John Wilkinson's rule before the outbreak of the Bishops' War, had as many as three hundred scholars on its books, 'of which number says Wood, ' were forty (or more) Masters of Art, but all mostly given to Calvinism Speaking with characteristic bitterness of these two halls, the same annalist observes, 'The said two places were therefore commonly styled the two nests of Precisians and Puritans Nor were New Inn Hall and Magdalen Hall the only scholastic houses that afforded shelter to Oxonians who were known to incline to Geneva rather than Canterbury. In spite of Laud's vigilance and severity against Precisians and scholars suspected of a leaning to non-conformity, puritanism was continually breaking out in the several colleges of the university.

And whilst the academic population of Oxford numbered several opponents of prelacy, and many scholars who, whilst approving episcopacy, were hotly averse to the high-church party, the 'laics' of the city were almost to a man against the bishops and in favour of the parliamentarian reformers of religion. In 1640 and the following year the politico-religious disposition of the town declared itself in tumultuous assemblies and riots, that reminded beholders of the days when the scholars and citizens were wont to slay one another under the walls of the hospices. Inspired with the insurrectionary spirit of the times the townsmen, exclaiming against the tyrannical usurpations of the university, questioned the privileges of the academic officers, insisted on their right to greater powers in the government of the city, sued 'privileged persons' in their municipal court, and flatly refused to fix the prices of candles and other commodities at the vice-chancellor's dictation. In January 1640-1, after preferring to the Lords in parliament what Antony Wood calls 'a malicious and insolent petition,' against the ancient or recently acquired privileges of the university, these contumacious laics rung their great bell in St Martin's, and would fain have occasioned a sanguinary riot, in behalf of a disreputable woman, whom the proctor was conveying to the spinning-house. The disturbance was renewed on the following night, to the music of St Martin's belfry and the indescribable terror of elderly ladies, when the timely intervention of the mayor and the capture of two principal misdemeanants prevented the row from growing to riot, 'although a great number continued in the street making great noises, and inciting others to rise, till about twelve of the clock at night'

Nor were these the most significant and terrifying indications of the state of laical feeling. When the university petitioned Parliament to preserve the cathedrals,, 'as affording a competent portion in an ingenuous way to many younger brothers of good parentage,' the more outrageous laics were heard to speak derisively of good parentage, and even to suggest that younger brothers should be provided for by an equitable division of their parents' estates. On hearing that Archbishop Laud had been sent to the Tower, the laics exhibited no signs of sorrow;—on the contrary, the beholder would have thought from the radiant cheerfulness of their countenances that some great good fortune had befallen the nation. And when the same imprisoned primate resigned (June 1641) his office of chancellor, the laics, in the diabolical insolency of their rebellious natures, instead of grieving that the university had lost so exemplary a chief, exclaimed that he had resigned none too soon, and that devout men would have grounds for thankfulness if the next chancellor should prohibit the wearing of copes in the collegiate chapels.

On the outbreak of hostilities between the sove-reign and the representatives of the people, Charles the First naturally looked to Oxford and Cambridge for large contributions to his inadequate means for carrying on a war in which the episcopal clergy were so peculiarly interested; and when, in the summer of 1642, he applied to them for substantial help, neither university surpassed the other in readiness to furnish him with pecuniary resources. Whilst the Cantabrigians brought together the cash and plate, which the Rev. Barnaby Oley and his coadjutors succeeded in conveying to the king, after eluding the force that, operating under Oliver Cromwell's personal command, had hoped to intercept the treasure near Lowler hedges, the Oxonians responded with appropriate alacrity to the letter in which the sovereign invited them to lend him money and precious metal at 8 per cent interest The royal application, addressed to Bishop Prideaux of Worcester, Vice-Chancellor of the University, was in the following terms:—

'Charles R.

' Reverend father in God, right truly and well beloved, we greet you well Whereas upon a false and scandalous pretence, and which we have sufficiently made appear to be such by our actions and declarations, and by the declaration of our Lords and Councellors here present with us, that we intended to make warre upon our Parliament: Horse is still levied, and plate and money is still brought in against, notwithstanding our declarations and proclamations to the contrary: which hath forced us, with a due regard to our safety and dignity, and to the peace of the kingdome, to desire the assistance of those good subjects for our necessary defence. And whereas our University of Oxford is not only involved in the consequences of such dangerous and illegal proceedings, equally with the rest of our sub-jects, but by our perpetuall care and protection of such nurseries of learning, we have especiall reason to expect their particular care of us, and their extraordinary assistance to our defence and preservation: These are therefore to will and require you to signifie to that our university, in such manner as shall appear to you best for our service, that any sums of money that either any of 6ur colleges, out of their treasuries, or any person thereof out of their particular fortunes, shall pay to this bearer, Dr. Richard Chaworth, and receive his receipt for the same, shall be received by us with interest of 8 per centum, justly and speedily as it shall please God to settle the distractions of this poore kingdome, of which our conscience bears us witness that we are not the cause. And so, not doubting but that our university will herein express her loyalty and affection to us, and that you will to your power assist us, so to hasten these expressions, as the truth of them might not be destroyed by the delay, we bid you heartily farewell. Given at our Court at Yorke, Julii the Seventh, Anno D'ni 1642

Immediately on the receipt of which letter, Con-vocation unanimously ordered that all monies then lying in the Savilian, Bodleian, and University chests, should forthwith be handed over to Dr. Cha-worth, who, in consequence of the order, received from the university chest 860I. — a sum that was speedily and largely augmented by the contributions of the colleges and individual academicians. But ere the king had touched the money of his loyal scholars, the Parliament had heard of their proceedings, and taken measures to check the current of supplies that had begun to flow from the universities to the crown. The vengeance of Parliament was soon felt by Cambridge, whose loyal scholars were subjected to a rigorous treatment that precluded them at the commencement of the war from making their university a stronghold of the royalist party. Nor were the Parliamentarians unmindful of the University of Oxford, though she was more fortunate than Cambridge in being allowed to retain the means of affording embarrassment to her enemies and succour to her friends in the martial struggle. An order was issued from Westminster for the apprehension of Doctors Prideaux, Fell, Frewen, and Potter—*i. e.* the Vice-Chancellor of the University, the Dean of Christ Church, the President of Magdalen College, and the Provost of Queen's— in order that they should answer for their 'high crime and conspiracy against the kingdome in bestirring themselves to collect the money and plate of the various academic societies, and transmit the said treasure to York, 'for maintaining of warrs against the Parliament and the whole kingdome, and endangering of religion and the liberties of the subject

For more than a year and a half the keener politicians of the country had been preparing, with greater or less secresy, for the appeal to arms, which shrewd and far-seeing observers of passing events had declared to be. inevitable from the first assembling of the Long Parliament. Even so early as January 1640-1, a body of a hundred and fifty Cavaliers had entered Oxford, and deposited at the Star Inn a quantity of arms and other ammunition, which occasioned a terrifying rumour amongst the Oxonian Puritans, that the murderous Papists were at their old tricks, and were bent on blowing up the city with gunpowder. But on the appearance of the Royal Proclamation (dated at York, Aug. 9,1642) for the suppression of the rebellion under the Earl of Essex, there no longer existed amongst the adherents of either party any need or power of concealing their belligerent purpose. Regiments were openly levied, and drilled in every part of the kingdom.

Antony Wood was a schoolboy in his tenth year when this proclamation was read in the Oxford market-place, on Saturday, Aug. 13, 1642,—a pro-ceeding speedily followed by military operations and excitements, that put a stop to the ordinary exercises of the superior schools, and so completely turned the heads of the children in the grammar-forms, that no threats or punishments could induce them to fix their attention on their tasks. To put the university in a condition to repel any Parliamentarian forces that might be sent against its members, Dr. Pinke, of New College, Dr. Prideaux's deputy in the vice-chancellor's office, summoned all the privileged men and their servants to appear before him in such armour as they could provide for the protection of themselves and the interests of learning. The men who mustered for review in obedience to this summons presented a motley and grotesquely various aspect. Some were furnished with complete suits of armour, and marched into the schools' quadrangle with soldierly pride in the brightness of their steel and the efficiency of their martial appurtenances. But many a valiant militiaman appeared with helmet and pike, but no breastplate, or with a serviceable musket, but no defensive accoutrements for his head or body. Together with raw serving-men, sent by their masters to trail a pike or carry a rusty gun at the review, there appeared comely undergraduates equipped for the display with swords of costume and cumbrous pistols.

But the military practice had not continued for many days before Alma Mater could point with pride to a strong and soldier-like corps. On the fifth day after the public reading of the proclamation, the available force of scholastic fighting-men, including scholars, collegiate and aularian servants, and the private servants of prosperous graduates, numbered three hundred and thirty; and ere forty-eight more hours had passed, the levy had attained the strength of four hundred and fifty men, divided into four squadrons—two of musketeers, one of pikemen, and a fourth of halberdiers. To bring this considerable and rapidly increasing force into order, and qualify it to act against experienced soldiers, the authorities found officers who sedulously trained the recruits to march and countermarch, to handle their weapons with dexterity, and wheel to right or left in unwavering lines. The quadrangles of Christ Church and New College became drill-yards, and resounded from morn to night with the exhilarating music of fifes and drums. Through rain and sunshine the soldiers daily took long marches out' in the neighbourhood of the university; and, leaving broken kettles to leak, and promising to repair the implements of peaceful industry at a more convenient season, the smiths of the town were incessantly employed in making pikes, repairing fire-arms, and relieving helmets and cuirasses of the consequences of neglect Other precautions also were taken for Alma Mater's safety. On the countryward end of Magdalen Bridge a barrier of long timber logs was erected to prevent hostile horsemen from entering the city ; and at the other extremity of the viaduct there was constructed a gate for the embarrassment of unwelcome visitors. Loads of stones were conveyed to the top of Magdalen Tower, in readiness to be hurled down upon any hostile force that should succeed in forcing the bridge. The other gates of the town were rendered extraordinarily secure with posts and chains; and an engineer, making a commencement of the military works which were soon to encompass the city of learning, set a numerous body of workmen to dig ' a crooked trench in the form of a bow across ' the highway at the end of St. John's College walks next the New Park, to hinder the entrance of any forces that should come that way ; at which place, as also at the East Bridge, was a very strict centinell kept every night.'

Whilst Parliamentarian troops were known to be passing through the country from London to Banbury and Warwick, and companies of Roundhead troopere scoured the Midland shires, every day had its exciting rumour or alarming intelligence for the Royalists of the university; but the first sharp and universal panic which the scholars experienced after withdrawing their attention from the subtleties of logic to the difficulties of military drill, originated in the surprise and terror of the sentinels, stationed along this same crooked trench, who mistook for a hostile force the two hundred troopers, who had been sent by Charles the King to protect his devoted collegians, and direct the measures for putting Oxford in a defensible condition. But though Sir John Byron, the colonel of the troopers, entered Oxford with the King's commission to provide for its safety, and met with an enthusiastic reception from the majority of the gownsmen, so soon as they had ascertained his friendliness, he suddenly evacuated the town after a lapse of some ten or twelve days, on hearing that Lord Say was approaching the university with, a considerable army. Upon the whole Sir John's brief stay with Alma Mater, which for a moment occasioned the loyal students lively satisfaction, affected the university prejudicially; for when his troop trotted out, of Oxford, it was swollen with nearly a hundred well-mounted recruits, Oxonians of wealth and influence, whom the war-fever, co-operating with the force of strong political convictions, had inspired to throw aside the gown and enlist as volunteers in the first regiment of cavalry that had appeared in their High Street, since the commencement of the war.

Scarcely had Sir John Byron's troopers departed, when the inhabitants of Oxford were informed of the approach of Colonel Goodwin's Parliamentarian troopers, who would speedily be followed by the new Lord-lieutenant of Oxfordshire, Lord Say. Goodwin's troopers conducted themselves with orderliness, but their Puritanism broke out in derisive comrents on the painted and idolatrous windows of Christ Church Cathedral, and the various Papistical devices which adorned the buildings of what the soldiers were pleased to call the arch-traitor Laud's nursery for mass-priests and Jesuits. Two days later appeared Lord Say, whose stay in the university gave the Oxonian loyalists an extremely unacceptable foretaste of the discipline which, a few years later, they endured at the hands of the rebellious and regicidal Parliament. Lord Say cannot be said to have treated the university with harshness. On the contrary, it has been charged against him that, had it not been for his leniency to academical malignants, and his culpable remissness in forbearing to plant a garrison in the town, in accordance with the entreaties of the Puritans of New Inn Hall, Oxford would not have become the stronghold of the Royalists after the battle of Edgehill. But, though innocent of violence or oppression towards the schoolmen, the Parliamentary peer occasioned lively chagrin and vehement exasperation to the dons, whose colleges he disarmed and searched for plate, and to whose military works he rendered the compliment of ordering that they should forthwith be destroyed.

One anecdote, taken from many authentic and reliable stories of a similar kind, is sufficient to illustrate the vexatious and comical ways in which the loyal scholars exhibited their contempt for Lord Say's authority during his occupation of their university. To none of the colleges which he ransacked for arms and treasure was the Lord Lieutenant more acrimoniously disposed than Christ Church, which, as the principal college of the malignant university, and as a house which had distinguished itself by zeal in raising the subscription for the royal exchequer, appeared to the Puritan peer chiefly accountable for the political feeling of the academic community. After a tedious search the guard of musketeers, appointed to relieve Christ Church of the contents of its treasury, came upon the strong chest which they were bent on rifling. Even then it was not till they had spent several minutes, and exerted their strength and mechanical ingenuity in breaking open the iron-plated box, that the irritated soldiers contrived to expose its interior, when to their rage they found lying at the bottom of the strong recep-tacle—a single great and a halter. The humorous collegian who, after withdrawing the collegiate purse from its usual resting-place, and in lieu of the abstracted treasure had provided the iron safe with a piece of rope and a hangman's fee, was Richard Allestree, whose important and courageous services in behalf of the exiled Stuarts secured for him the provostship of Eton on the restoration of Charles the Second.

After this unsatisfactory inspection of the Christ Church chest, the visitors went to the deanery, where they gathered into a particular room all the plate and other valuable chattels which they designed to remove from the malignant collega Having thus put the spoil into a strongly-locked apartment, they retired to their quarters for the night, confident that on the following morning they should find the booty where they had placed it. The event, however, failed to justify their confidence; for on revisiting the deanery at an early hour of the next day they discovered that some enemy, possessing duplicate keys to the dean's lodgings, had entered, the residence during the night, and abstracted the chattels which they had been at so much pains to collect. On learning that Allestree was the person who had thus baffled and held them up to ridicule on two separate occasions, the military inquisitors took the precaution of arresting the Royalist divine before they renewed their search for the property which had so vexatiously escaped from their custody,

Having learnt the necessity for caution and vigi-lance, the Parliamentarian officers continued their search for arms and treasure in a more methodical manner, stationing guards at the gates of the con-tumacious colleges, and at the doors of private dwellings, whose inmates were known to be enthu-siastic supporters of the royal cause, so that articles of value could not be removed from them. Magdalen, Merton, New, Corpus, Christ Church, University, and other colleges, were speedily deprived of their plate and military munitions. To replace the scholastic volunteers, who were disbanded and relieved of their weapons, Say and Sale enrolled a regiment of citizens, who displayed significant alacrity in offering to bear arms in behalf of the Parliament. And having thus reduced the scholars to impotency, and put them under the foot of the town, the Puritan commander, whose head-quarters were at the Star Hotel, illminated the street in front of his temporary residence with a bon-fire of books and pictures, gathered from the churches and the houses of the Church Papists.

Having thus taken possession of Oxford, it was of course the intention of the Parliament to retain it in their hands ; but the military exigencies of the crisis interfering with the designs of the Westminster Council, Lord Say was compelled to relinquish the stronghold of learning and loyalty, and hasten to the field with the forces which during his occupation of the university had become a small army. President Rogers, of New Inn, speaking in the interest of the academical Puritans and their civic allies, implored the commander not to retire from the city without leaving in it a garrison sufficiently strong to secure it against the Royalists, and to protect godly and well-affected persons from the violence of the malignants. But Say and Sele had no power to comply with the reasonable request of the Puritans. After addressing the two parties of Oxonian residents, in language calculated to depress the Cava-liers and inspire the Parliamentarians with confidence in the ability of Essex to drive their antagonists from the field, Lord Say withdrew his soldiers from the city,— after having destroyed the inadequate military works of the Royalist soldiers. The greater part of the plate collected by his searchers was restored to the colleges from which it had been taken, on the understanding that they would produce it for the use of the Parliament whenever they should be required to do so. Christ Church alone was so unfortunate as not to recover her plate from Lord Say, who punished her vexatious opposition to his authority by carrying off that portion of her treasure which it had cost him so much trouble and annoyance to lay hands upon. But whilst thus generous to the colleges, in respect to their plate, the Puritan peer was careful to place beyond their reach the arms and warlike munitions which he had taken from the gownsmen, and of which the Parliamentarian soldiers were in urgent need.

CHAPTER V.

THE CAVALIERS IN OXFORD.

WHILST the more sanguine supporters of the Parliament were congratulating themselves on the fight of Edgehill,—or Keynton Battle, as it was for a while more generally called,—the survivors of the Cavalier army, which had fought in that stubborn and sanguinary contest under Charles's personal observation, were marching into Oxford, with a gallant show of triumphant satisfaction with a battle, in which they had taken some seventy colours from the enemy, and had inflicted such losses on the Puritan army, as left the Roundheads in no condition to follow up the dubious advantage which they magnified boastfully into a signal, though indecisive, victory.

The king and his two sons, Charles and James (lads who, even in the days when

Oxford had mere children on her roll of students, were almost too young for undergraduates), Prince Rupert, who had commanded at Edgehill, and Prince Maurice, were in the van of the Royalist forces, that entered the university on the 29th of October, 1652, with a prudent display of the colours recently taken from Roundhead regiments, and to the tunes of military bands whose music combined, with the acclamations of the fickle mob, that had cheered Say's troopers a few weeks earlier just as uproariously, to stir the hearts of beholders, and inspire them with confidence in a cause whose defenders could look so bravely and rejoice so theatrically. At Penniless Bench the. mayor of the Parliamentarian borough offered his sovereign fair words, which Charles was too wary to believe, and money which he was very glad to pocket; and at Christ Church the monarch in arms, at the head of his not vanquished army, was appropriately received with Latin talk and the usual observances of ancient etiquette Henceforth, till the capitulation, Oxford was a camp rather than a seat of learning.

The soldiers of the royal army were billeted on the colleges and the houses of citizens. The twenty-seven pieces of ordnance, which the king had brought off from Keynton-field, were driven to the grove of Magdalen College, which became the chief barrack of the artillerymen, whilst New College was converted into a magazine of arms and furniture. Undoing whatever remained of Say's military operations, the Royalists disarmed the citizens and restored weapons to the loyal scholars, who forthwith reconstituted themselves in companies for the king's service. Competent engineers bestirred themselves to surround the city with defensive works, and in order that their undertakings might not fail through want of labour, stringent orders were issued by which gownsmen and townsmen were constrained to work with pick and spade, or pay money that would find efficient substitutes to work for them, Christ Church became the king's palace, whence the ordinary occupants of studious chambers were required to retreat, so that his majesty's courtiers and counsellors might have quarters befitting their dignity. A powder-mill was set to work at Oseney; and New Inn, from which President Rogers's Puritan students had fled to the country on the approach of the Cavalier army, was appropriated to the moneyers and mechanicians of the same mint, that had for several years minted silver for the king at Aberystwith, and subsequently at Shrewsbury and York

On her arrival at Oxford, in the following year, Merton was assigned to Henrietta Maria,—or Queen Mary, as she was universally called by her loyal adherents and the commonalty of the country. After the opening of the first law-term of 1642-3, the Lord-Keeper heard causes in the Convocation House, whither the custodian of the royal conscience brought the Great Seal, which the Parliamentarians had counterfeited, after the well-mounted and tippling braggart, Elliot, had conveyed the Clavis Regni from London to York at full gallop. Sir Thomas Aylesbury, as one of the Masters of the Court of Bequests, sat at the same time in the Natural Philosophy School, to hear the applications and adjudicate on the claims of suitors. And when, a twelvemonth later, the perplexed and un-teachable king summoned his faithful Lords and Commons to deliberate with him on the affairs of the nation, the Lords were provided with a chamber in the schools, and the representatives of the Commons with seats in the Convocation House, to which places for debate and legislative enactment the two branches of the Cavalier parliament retired, after they had listened to the gracious speech which his Majesty delivered to them from his throne in Christ Church Hall.

No sooner had the Cavaliers taken possession of Oxford than Royalists of all ages and both sexes, and every degree of gentility, flocked to the university from nearly every quarter of the kingdom,—but chiefly from the midland and southern shires. Clergy ejected from their benefices by Parliamentary violence, Royalist squires whose manor-houses and farms had fallen into the hands of the enemy, peers who, after trimming between the rival factions, determined to take their chance with the party which comprised the majority of the high aristocracy, soldiers of fortune eager to make professional capital out of the national troubles, boys burning with chivalric enthusiasm for a sovereign contending against rebellious subjects, wives and mothers tortured with anxiety for the welfare of their impoverished families, and girls too ignorant of adversity and too much elated by the excitements of new events and novel experiences to realize the sorrows of the crisis or see what grounds their parents had for dejection. Of such various kinds were the gentle people who betook themselves to Oxford, with all the money, plate, and other portable treasure on which they could lay their hands, before setting out from the homes to which many of them never returned. Not a few of the refugees reached the university in a condition of impoverishment which rendered them sources of weakness rather than of strength to the population of the overcrowded city. But the poorest of them made a brave effort to endure misfortune cheerfully, and derive amusement from their calamitous plight. A few days after Peter Heylyn arrived at Oxford in his coach and horses, which had conveyed him from Hampshire to the schools, he was asked by an acquaintance on what he contrived to support existence. 'Horseflesh and old leather,' replied the Royalist divine, who had sold his carriage and animals to raise funds for his immediate exigencies in a city where all the necessaries of life had become very dear.

It might be supposed that, under the cares and distractions of a period which loaded him with vexa-tious business and weighty cares, Charles had neither the time nor humour to smile upon learning; but on the first day of November, following his arrival in Oxford, there was celebrated in compliance with his orders a pompous creation of more than two hundred graduates, whom he was pleased to invest with the insignia of scholarship, in his inability to endow them with more substantial gifts. Eighteen doctors and forty-eight bachelors of divinity, thirty-four doctors and fourteen bachelors of civil law, five doctors and eight bachelors of physic, seventy-six masters and twelve bachelors of arts, were thus made out of the courtiers and adventurers whom the sovereign's misfortunes had gathered to the schools; and in the confusion which attended this wholesale manufacture of unlearned scholars, towards the close of a dismal November day, Wood assures us that '.some were so impudent as to thrust themselves (when it grew dark) into the hands of him that presented, to be created, being not all mentioned in the catalogue of those that were signed by the king.'

For awhile every Royalist fugitive from the shires on reaching the university, if he had not previously obtained academic rank, solicited the sovereign for a letter, requiring the vice-chancellor to confer a specified degree upon the bearer, who would thereby acquire the dignity of a graduate in addition to the privileges of academic affiliation; and the king, no* thing loth to confer favours which cost him nothing but the trouble of writing his signature, gratified the applicants for scholastic rank so indiscreetly, that on Friday, Feb. 3, 1642-3, he was petitioned by convocation to refrain from an exercise of his prerogative which threatened to lower Oxonian honours in public estimation. Whereupon Charles ordered that henceforth ' no scholar, intending to make benefit of his degree, should have any recommendations from him, or, if recommended, should thereby have or enjoy any honour or benefit of any degree, unless he should be found capable of the same by the statutes of the university, and give caution to perform his exercises and pay all usual fees.'

But, apart from the wholesale creation of Latin-less graduates, the scholastic business of the university languished and almost ceased soon after the entry of the Cavaliers. A few scholars, whilst discharging their military duties, found time to perform the ceremonies requisite for the attainment of degrees; but in the three years, from 1643-4 to 1645-6 inclusive, only one hundred and forty-nine students, less than fifty per *annum*, assumed the B. A. hood and title. Lectures ceased to be delivered in the public schools; acts were no longer celebrated ; and before Henrietta Maria's arrival in the university, in July 1643, there was not a tutor in Oxford who had a class of sophists to instruct Even so early as November, 1642, the New College Grammar-school for children was removed from its old quarters to the dark choristers' chamber at the east end of the Common Hall, in order that the cloister and tower of the college might be used safely as a gunpowder-magazine; and at the opening of the next year several of the children, who had hitherto attended the school, were sent out of Oxford to places where they might be educated with a regularity no longer attainable in Oxonian classrooms.

Neglect of learning prevailed throughout the university, where work over books was exchanged for toil in the trenches, and attendance in collegiate chapels was no longer required of undergraduates who complied with martial discipline in learning the exercises of the drill-ground The students for the most part vacated their rooms within collegiate walls for lodgings in the town, in order that the colleges might afford accommodation to the wealthier of the Cavalier visitors who, by the large rents which they paid for comfortable quarters, enabled the principals and fellows of the scholastic houses to render the heavy sums which they were required to furnish for the defence of the city and the prosecution of the war. Nor were the colleges singular in deriving pecuniary gain from the Cavalier aristocracy, whose disbursements enriched the civic tradesmen, who, whilst behaving with prudent submissive-ness to the court in arms, secretly favoured the Parliament.

In the first week of June, 1643, it was ordained that every scholar or other person lodging in any college or hall, being of an age between sixteen and sixty years, should labour personally on the public works one entire day per week, or pay twelve pence to the royal treasury for every day that he avoided his appointed share of the general toil And on June 21, 1643, ' His Majesty, for the better furthering of the fortifications, did desire and require the principal governor of every college to appoint, one or more of the officers or servants of the colleges, upon notice given to them of the day from the commissioners for working, to give notice to all scholars and lodgers in the college, to observe their day, and to deliver a true note of their names to the commissioners under their hands, to appoint one in every college to collect the monies of the defaulters, and pay it over to the treasurer appointed to receive it, and a true note of those that neither work nor pay for their defaults. Half the colleges and the halls were to work on Monday, and the other half on Tuesday, from six to eleven in the morning, and from one to six at night, and every person to bring his tool with him,'

Though the above order makes it clear that the collegiate and aularian residents were not altogether innocent of a disposition to shirk the toil of making trenches and earthworks, there is good reason for believing that the defaulters were seldom gownsmen. The scholars — alike tutors and undergraduates — appear to have set an example of military zeal and punctual industry to the promiscuous multitude gathered with the town. Wood assures us 'that from the beginning of the war' till the capitulation of Oxford, ' the generality of the scholars were very loyal to the crown, and did the best and most exact service of any during the time that Oxford was a garrison;' and that' there were several also of them that were not only officers of the garrison, but also in the king's army, disposed in several places in England, who for their loyalty to the last ought to have their names commended to posterity And, writing in the same spirit and to the same purpose in *The Life of Richard All-estree, D.D.,* Bishop Fell observes: Having recovered a little strength, he' (*i. e.* Allestree) ' was engaged to employ it in military service, the exigence of his Majesty's affairs calling for the aid of all his loyal subjects, and in particular the scholars; and accordingly a regiment of them was raised, who served as volunteers without any pay or reward, and performed all duties not only in the garrison, and sallied for the defence of it in case of attacks and sieges, but were also commanded upon parties abroad, and endured the fatigue of marches and ill-treatment of mean quarters, differing in nothing from the poor mercenary soldier besides their civility and justice to the country-folk while they stayed with them, and paying them at departure: things so unusual, that when, at their going off from quarters, they offered their landlords money, they imagined it was done in jest and abuse, and at last, by finding it left with them, were convinced that it was done in earnest. In this regiment Mr. Allestree, though a master of arts and fellow of the college, thought it no disgrace to carry a musket and perform all the duties of a common soldier, forward upon all occasions to put himself into action; and in this service he continued until the unhappy end of the war.'

At the time of its capitulation, the Oxford garrison comprised ' three auxiliary regiments, consisting of gentlemen and their servants, scholars, citizens, and inhabitants, who were not properly of the garrison in pay ; one of which regiments was the Caroline ' Devil's Own,' composed principally of the lawyers and their servants, whose original colonel was Lord-Keeper Littleton.

But though Oxonians went in heartily for the perilous excitements and labours of warfare, enduring privations patiently, and distinguishing themselves by gallantry in the field, it is certain that they suffered deplorably from the demoralizing pleasures of camps and the influence of a discipline which permitted them to seek in certain most pernicious kinds of license a compensation for the hardships entailed upon them by the rigour of martial government Many a lad who had been a studious and virtuous undergraduate before the battle of Edgehill died of delirium tremens, or contracted incurable habits of sottishness before the dispersion of the auxiliary regiments. When Antony Wood returned (in the autumn of 1646) to Oxford from Thame, where he was put to school soon after Edgehill fight, he heard gloomy stories of the havoc which war had made with the morals of the academic youth. After his return to the house of his nativity says the annalist in his autobiography, ' he found Oxford empty, as to scholars, but pretty well replenished with Parliamentarian soldiers. Many of the inhabitants had gained great store of wealth from the court and Royalists, that had for several years continued among them ; but as for the young men of the city and university, he found many of them to have been debauched by bearing arme3 and doing the duty belonging to soldiers, as watching, warding, and sitting in tipling-houses for whole nights together

In like manner, describing the condition of the scholastic youth at the close of the war, the same writer observes, in *The Annals*:—' Those few also that were remaining were, for the most part, especially such that were young, much debauched, and become idle by their bearing arms and keeping company with rude soldiers. Much of their precious time was lost by being upon the guard night after night, and by doing those duties which appertained to them as bearers of arms, and so consequently had opportunities, as lay-soldiers had, of gaming, drinking, swearing, &c., as notoriously ap-peared to the Visitors that were sent by the Parliament to reform the university. The truth is, that they (I blame not all) were so guilty of those vices, that those that were looked upon as good wits, and of great parts at their first coming, were, by strange inventions (not now to be named) to entice them to drinking, and to be drunk, totally lost and rendered useless. I have had the opportunity (I cannot say happiness) to peruse several songs, ballads, and such-like frivolous stuff, that were made by some of the ingenious sort of them while they kept guard at the Hollybush and Angel, near Rowley, in the west suburbs; which, though their humour and chiefest of their actions are in them described, yet I shall pass them by, as very unworthy to be here, or any part, mentioned.' When we find a writer, who abhorred the Parliament and detested the Soundheads, speaking thus severely of the dissoluteness and depravity of the lads who spent their money, strength, and health in the King's service, we may be sure that their misdemeanours defied the arts of palliation.

Whilst the war proved thus destructive of the morality, it was not less injurious to the finances of the scholars, who, in addition to the heavy payments drawn from them by taxation, were compelled to send to the Mint whatever articles of plate they were known to retain in their possession. The silver which Lord Say had remitted to the colleges on withdrawing his troops from the university was all paid to the King's moneyers; and besides many hundreds of pounds of the precious metal thus absorbed by the factory of coin, the scholars and private individuals connected with the scholastic houses placed at the King's disposal their drinking-cups and other articles of the same metal, which they had received as heirlooms from their ancestors, and had hoped to transmit as heirlooms to their descendants.

For more than two centuries it has been the fashion of writers to applaud the colleges for thus generously, and of their free-will, making over to the Bang an amount of treasure which, it is implied, they would have been allowed to keep had they been less loyally disposed. In the same manner the private contributors have been extolled for patriotic munificence and disinterested devotion to their sovereign's cause, because they subscribed to exactions which they were powerless alike to avoid or to resist. There is, however, abundant testimony that these eulogies are misapplied. In the struggle, which was far more their own quarrel than that of the King, the Oxonian ecclesiastics naturally helped to their umost the sovereign who had sacrificed so much for them, and in spite of his reluctant concessions to the Puritans was known to be at heart a cordial approver of Laudian principles. Small credit for unselfish loyalty is due to the men who in lending to the King were merely giving to themselves.

The case of a considerable proportion of the private and laical contributors differed from that of the majority of the clerical subscribers. Even when they were sincere adherents of the Crown, they had not those personal and substantial interests in the quarrel which would have necessarily disposed them to fight it out to their last shilling. But though their material concern in the struggle was comparatively trivial, they were constrained to give no less largely than the partisans who had provoked the contest which was being fought especially in their behalf In plain words, they were stript of their silver chattels; and their plunder was none the less positive and galling, because a courtly fiction represented that they gave out of benevolence what was taken from them by force,—or, to speak precisely, what they knew well would be taken from them by force if they ventured to assert their right to retain it. The Stuarts were clever in disguising their extortions with specious words. An illegal seizure of money they called a benevolent payment, an arbitrary extortion they termed a loan. And when the object was to raise funds for the Civil War, Charles and his Queen regarded themselves as having an indefeasible right to pounce on everything that came within the reach of their hands, so long as they declared themselves merely the borrowers of the appropriated articles, which they would of course repay at their earliest convenience. When Henrietta Maria took possession of Boynton Hall, the seat of the Puritan Sir William Strickland, on her way from Burlington to Oxford, she repaid her entertainers by walking off with a quantity of plate, which she had no more right than any other depredator to appropriate. The terms with which the royal freebooter dressed up this act of open plunder, perpetrated in the absence of the owner of the property, are recorded by Sir William's descendant, Miss Agnes Strickland, who appears to reflect with pleasure on the Queen's condescension in thus ' borrowing for his Majesty's use' what no one then present at Boynton Hall was authorized to lend her. At Oxford, plate was borrowed in like manner, on the understanding that it was taken only as a loan which would of course be repaid with interest on the first suitable occasion. With a conciseness that is not without a ring of asperity, Antony Wood records how the gifts made to him by his godfathers and godmother at his christening were swept off to New Inn by the executors of his Majesty's commands. ' This yeare,' says the autobiographer, under date 1643, 'the plate which had been given to A. Wood, by his godfathers and godmother, which was considerable, was (with all other plate in Oxon) *carried by his Majesty's command* to the mint at New Inne, and then turned into money to pay his Majestie's armies.'

Charles's proclamation for establishing the mint at Oxford was dated Dec. 15, 1642, in anticipation of the arrival of the waggons and carts which, on the third day of the following month, brought to the university the plant and workmen of the coining establishment which had for some time been at work at Shrewsbury. Other coiners and tools for minting money arrived from York; and with all possible expedition the manufacturers of cash went to work in New Inn, under the direction of Thomas Bushell, formerly the farmer of the royal mines in the principality of Wales, the initial letter of whose surname appears on some of the coins uttered by the Oxford mint, which was (as we have before observed) the Welsh mint transferred to the English university. Of the money that issued from this establishment the greater part bore the design of the Welsh or Prince of Wales's Feathers,—a mark that indicated at the same time the history of the factory and the nationality of the principal workmen. The money also bore other signs of the circumstances of its manufacture. A crown-piece issued by the master of the New Inn mint has the word ' Oxon' under the King's horse, and a view of Oxford surrounded by entrenchments. The ' B' of Richard Baylie, President of St. John's College, appears on much of the silver put into circulation in 1644 ; and though some of Thomas Bushell's coins are of fine execution and sterling value, the coarseness and metallic impurity of others indicate the difficulties which the mint-master experienced in getting fresh supplies of skilful workmen, and the expedients to which the scarcity of silver and the King's urgent need of money compelled him to have recourse. But of all the distinguishing marks visible on money that proceeded from the New Inn mint, none is more characteristic of the crisis or familiar to Englishmen of the present day than the legend,' Exurgat Deus Dissipentur Inimici: Let God arise and let his enemies be scattered which appears on the coins popularly designated 'exurgat money

Mint-master Bushell having planted his men and machinery at New Inn Hall, the King on January 10, 1642-3, sent letters to the colleges and halls, requiring that they should without delay send their plate to the mint, so that it might forthwith be converted into money. It is scarcely credible that a copy of this demand was served on the society of New Inn, where the coiners had established themselves, and no scholar remained who could -be regarded as the official representative of the Puritan nest. In the absence of President Rogers and his precise pupils, who had withdrawn from Oxford on the coming of the Cavaliers, the society of New Inn had for the time ceased to exist, whilst the Royalist government held possession of its building. Antony Wood, therefore, must have been animated by a spirit of scornful and vindictive irony when he remarked that New Inn distinguished herself from all the other scholastic houses of the university by forbearing to send plate to the mint of the distressed sovereign.

The other academic houses, acting probably in ac-cordance with the prevailing sentiment of their mem-bers, did what they would have been forced to do, however much they had wished to do otherwise. Charles gained possession of the silver which Lord Say had imprudently restored to the colleges. Christ Church had lost her domestic plate, but she sent to New Inn the sacred vessels and silver ornaments of her Cathedral Church. The plate deposited at the mint on January 20, 1642-3, by Christ Church, Jesus, Oriel, Queen's, Lincoln, University, Brasen Nose, Magdalen, All Soul's, Balliol, Mer-ton, and Trinity, amounted to 1610 lbs. 1 oz. 18 dwts. Pembroke and Wadham, young colleges that had not yet arrived at the dignity of owning a plate-chest, had no silver goods to contribute; but the loyalty of the Pembrokians and Wadhamites is beyond suspicion. Exeter College alone was affected by doubts whether she could conscientiously give up the plate of which she was merely the trustee; but these scruples having yielded to the pressure most likely to dissipate fanciful notions concerning the sovereign's right to do whatever he liked, the society of the tender consciences followed in the wake of the other scholastic houses, and conveyed to New Inn, February 2, 1643, plate amounting in weight to 246 lbs. 8 oz. 1 dwt. At the same time individual contributors, with doleful countenances, surrendering on loan what they can scarcely have hoped ever to recover, yielded 701 lbs. 10 oz. 9 dwts. of silver. Thus the exaction drew to the royal coffers nearly two thousand five hundred and sixty ounces of plate,—an amount so inadequate to the royal needs that it is difficult to mention it without a smile. Small though it was, this forced loan, however, afforded considerable aid to the Cavaliers who fought in days when a little money went a long way.

CHAPTER VI

HENRIETTA MARIA'S TRIUPH AND OXFORD'S CAPITULATION.

SOME of the gloomiest and most anxious days of Charles the First's life were passed during the interval between the battle of Edgehill and Henrietta Maria's arrival in the university, which he had entered with all the external signs of triumph and confidence, and from which he eventually retreated in the garb and disguise of a gentle serving-man, riding behind his master. The loyalty of the scholars and the brave assurances of his principal adherents could not disguise the gravity of the crisis, or blind him to the probability that the struggle into which he had drifted would prove alike disastrous to his crown and his family. Not that events had altogether dissipated the delusions which had brought him thus far to his ruin. In moments of comparative elation — or rather, let us say, in moments of comparative freedom from depressing anticipations—he still regarded himself as the viceregent of the Almighty, and derived an increase of resoluteness from the fond conceits which encouraged him to believe that the impious rebellion of his misguided subjects was nothing more than a transient social distemper, which would yield to remedial treatment and the force of their natural affections. For why had he been endowed with regal divinity, and appointed by the Creator of the universe to be a king of men, if his divine quality and the authority of his sacred commission were of no avail against the directors of a wicked insurrection?

Two years of stern and startling experiences had, however, wrought such a change in the baffled King that in the absence of the Queen, whom he feared scarcely less than he loved her, he would fain have made such terms with his adversaries as would have given them the substance of their demands, whilst depriving the regal office of no salutary privilege or real honour. But though his evil genius could not approach his council-chamber personally, she was near enough to him to be well aware of his hesitations in despotic stubbornness and his inclinations to prudence, and to counteract the influence of his more judicious advisers and his own wiser deliberations, Knowing how much alliteration aids a scornful tone in firing weak natures to insolence, she had styled the Lords and Commons assembled at Westminster ' the perpetual Parliament;' and she declared that, though no one surpassed her in longing for peace, she would consent to no arrangements for pacification which were not preluded by ' the disbanding of the perpetual Parliament.' Writing from the north, she threatened to leave England for ever, and settle in France, if her husband presumed to make peace with the rebels and disband his army before there had been brought about' an end of this perpetual Parliament And whilst approaching Oxford, in her memorable march from York to the university, the ' she-majesty generalissima as she delighted to describe herself, at the head of an army of three thousand infantry and thirty companies of cavalry, ridiculed her husband's cowardly apprehensions, and disdainfully insisted that he should ' do what he had resolved upon

Elated by the results of her visit to Holland, exulting in the manifestations of loyalty which her residence in Yorkshire had occasioned, and intoxicated by the more brilliant than material successes which her activity and cleverness and beauty had brought to the royal cause, the wilful and overbearing woman was in no humour to listen to moderate proposals, when Charles marched forth in gallant array from Oxford, and met her in Warwickshire, hard by the field where the battle of Edgehill had been won by both of the opposed armies. Prattling gaily about the incidents of her military progress from the north, as though the civil war were little more than a court-pageant got up by law-students for her amusement, she protested that she would not lay aside her sword until she had driven the Roundheads from Westminster, and taught the chiefs of the perpetual Parliament a lesson which neither they nor their descendants should speedily forget. The Queen of England was the daughter of Henry Quatre of France, and the rebels should rue the day when they took it into their stupid noddles that they could make her less than a queen. Was there any man who heard her and dared advise her to make peace with the insurgents on terms that would be derogatory to her honour,—and her husband's ? And of all the men who listened to the petulant and fascinating creature, whilst she poured forth her pretty bravados, none was less able to curb her spirit and give her the light of common sense than the puzzled, faint-featured, stammering gentleman whom wifely duty vainly enjoined her to obey.

Her sons, Charles and James, had accompanied
their father from Oxford to Keynton Vale, when the weak husband and ungovernable wife met again after a separation of about seventeen months; and, when the King's guard of troopers had ranged themselves with the escort that had attended the she generalissima from Stratford-upon-Avon, Henrietta Maria saw that the military pomp of her public entrance into the university would not fall short of the splendour and picturesqueness proper to so momentous an incident in her royal

career.

From the preparations for her reception nothing had been omitted which could give expression to the loyalty of the university, and the delight with which the Oxonians welcomed her to Merton. 'The soldiers says Wood, ' were placed on each side of the streets with their muskets charged, as well to enlarge as guard their passage; and behind them every house near which she passed was thronged with spectators to behold her. In the first place went the carriages for the removal of the court; then followed the servants' troop, commanded by Sir Will. Killigrew; after them his Majesty's gentlemen pensioners, and others of their Majesties' servants and domestic officers, the trumpets and the loud music all sounding as they passed along; next came the heralds in their embroidered coats, of whom Garter, coming last, was accompanied on the right hand by the mayor of Oxon in his scarlet, and mace upon his shoulder. After them came serjeants-at-arms, bearing maces; and next, immediately before their Majesties, the Earl of Forth, lord-general of his Majesty's army, and the Earl of Dorset, lord-chamberlain of her Majesty's house hold Prince Rupert and the Duke of Richmond rid on that side of the coach on which their Majesties sate; and in the rear of all followed the gentlemen of his Majesty's troop. At Quatervois, through which she passed, the citizens entertained her with an English speech, delivered by Mr. Timothy Carter, the town-clerk, in the name of the city, and presented her with a purse of gold. At Christ Church she was received by the vice-chancellor and heads of the houses in their scarlet. From thence she was conducted by the King to Merton College, by a back way made for that purpose through one of the canons' gardens, another belonging to Corpus Christi, and then through Merton College Grove. When she came to her lodging (that belonging to the wardens of the same college) she was entertained with an oration by Strode, orator of the university. That being done, a book of printed verses in Latin and English, which were made by the students of the university to welcome her arrival into England, were, with a rich pair of gloves, presented to her in the name of the university.'

Notwithstanding the scarcity of precious metal, the moneyers at New Inn produced, in honour of the occasion, a silver medal adorned with artistic devices and a legend which represented that the rebellion was at its last gasp, and that their Majesties, who had met under favourable omens in Keynto Vale, July 13, 1643, were objects of especial concern to the sun, moon, and stars. On the obverse of the medal a dragon, symbolical of impious insurrection, lies dead at the feet of the royal pair; and the inscription on the reverse describes their meeting as an ' omen of victory and peace

From July 13, 1643, to April 3, 1644,—a period little short of nine months, during which, Charles, after neglecting opportunities and rejecting overtures for an amicable settlement of affairs with the 'perpetual parliament saw his prospects lose that delusive appearance of returning prosperity which had helped to subject him to his wife's disastrous counsels against thoughts of peace,—Henrietta Maria presided over a court in Merton College, whither the gentlewomen of Cavalier families hastened to bask in the smiles and dread the frowns of their impulsive and capricious mistress. It was at Abingdon, on the latter of the above-mentioned dates, that Charles took his last farewell of the wife, whom he loved as passionately as weak men usually love the women whose insolence and rashness bring them to ruin. Strangely had Henrietta altered for the worse in outward aspect during her sojourn in Oxford. She had entered the university in the brightness of beauty and the full play of buoyant spirits. An anxious, sorrow-stricken woman, broken in pride and bodily health, she was scarcely recognizable as the ' she-generalissima who marched triumphantly from Yorkshire to the midland counties, when she journeyed unostentatiously from Abingdon to the west country, whence, after enduring acute sickness at Bath, and giving birth to a princess at Exeter, she escaped to her native land, where, upon the death of the fond husband for whose destruction she was in no small degree accountable, she was thankful to hide her grief and shame in a convent.

After the Queen's departure for the west, the decline of Charles's fortunes was rapid. Marston Moor, the second battle of Newbury, and the decisive battle of Naseby reduced the Royalists to a condition of weakness and defeat from which no efforts, possible to their shattered and demoralized troops, could raise their cause; and before two full years had elapsed since he had torn himself from Henrietta Maria at

Abingdon, the fallen monarch saw that for all practical ends his desperate game of resistance had been played out, though a few of his more stubborn adherents might protract the bootless struggle for months or even for years. On May 5, 1646, he surrendered his person to the Scotch army lying before Newark, an event speedily followed by the capitulation of the Oxford garrison.

Numbering some five thousand soldiers, strongly entrenched and occupying a powerful city, possessing thirty-eight pieces of ordnance, seventy barrels of powder, two powder-mills, and provisions for an eight months' siege, the garrison of Oxford was in a position to command honourable terms, when it consented to surrender to the greatly superior and rapidly increasing forces under Sir Thomas Fairfax. And though the fall of their stronghold occasioned much bitter dissatisfaction to those of the scholars and other Cavaliers who, over-rating the strength of the fortifications and the means available for the defence of the city, murmured against the surrender, none of them could deny that the Royalist commissioners had done their best to relieve the submission of the ignominy of defeat. By the fifth of the ' Articles concluded and agreed for the surrender of Oxford and Farringdon,' it was stipulated, 'That Sir Thomas Glemham, Knight, Governor of Oxford, with his servants and all that to him belongs, and all officers and soldiers of horse and foot, and of the train of artillery (as well reformed officers and soldiers as others) with their servants, and all that pertains to them, shall march out of the city of Oxon, with their horses and compleat arms that properly belong unto them, proportionable to their past and present commands, flying colours, trumpets sounding, drums beating, matches lighted at both ends, bullet in their mouths, and every soldier to have twelve charges of powder, match and bullet proportionable, and with bag and baggage, to any place within fifteen miles of Oxford, which the governor shall choose, where such of the common soldiers as desire to go to their own homes and friends, shall lay down their arms, and shall be delivered up to such as the General, Sir Thomas Fairfax, shall appoint to receive them By the same article it was further declared,' That those of the three auxiliary regiments, consisting of gentlemen and their servants, scholars, citizens and inhabitants, who are not properly of the garrison in pay; and such reformed officers and soldiers who shall not be willing to march forth, shall not be forced to march out by this article, but shall have the benefit of the following articles, to remove or remain in Oxford, and in all things also which may concern them; and those also, who shall march forth, shall have the benefit of the ensuing articles in all things, except for remaining in Oxford

Seldom has Oxford seen a more dismal day than June 24, 1646, on which the Cavalier garrison went through the humiliating ceremony of surrendering to the victorious Parliamentarians. From the early dawn till the close of the long summer's day it rained violently and incessantly, so that of the drenched and miserable infantry who marched from Magdalen Bridge to Shotover Hill, between two lines of Sir Thomas Fairfax's troops, the soldier was an exceptionally fortunate fellow who preserved a serene mind under afflicting circumstances. Prince Rupert and Prince Maurice, together with the nobility and principal gentlemen of the garrison, had ridden out of the town on the morning of the previous Monday. Other Cavaliers of high degree, attended by their servants, had trotted out of town on the following day. These two separate parties of retiring Royalists, added together, did not fall short of three hundred horsemen. The two thousand soldiers of the auxiliary regiments, escaping the degradation of the public ' march out remained in their quarters till the conquering force had taken possession of the city, when, on laying down their arms in compliance with the terms of the treaty of capitulation, they were supplied with ' passes authorizing them to travel to their various homes in different parts of the kingdom, or were permitted for a while to live quietly within the liberties of the university. Moreover, on the day of the general evacuation, between five hundred and a thousand Cavaliers,—private persons who, without being enrolled in regiments, had aided in the defence of the city, and enlisted soldiers, who wished to retire through the north-gate on their way towards Yorkshire and Gloucestershire,—were allowed to leave the captured stronghold without contributing to the principal spectacle of the surrender. But more than two thousand fighting-men moved over Magdalen Bridge in the presence of the Puritan chiefs, and towards Shotover between lines of Roundhead infantry, to the music of their drums and trumpets, and with whatever display of colours was practicable under the torrents of rain which beat against every outstretched banner, and caused every streamer to hang dolefully against its staff

Towards the close of this rainiest day of an un-usually rainy summer, the infantry who had thus quitted the loyal university entered Thame, drenched to the skin, weary, and befouled with mud. Antony Wood, then an inmate of the Thame vicarage, whilst he learnt grammar at the free-school of the town, conversed with several of the poor fellows, the majority of whom lost no time in plying the only trade for which they had a taste in the service of foreign powers. ' In the evening of the said day,' the annalist says in his autobiography,' many of the king's foot-partie, that belonged to the said garrison, came into Thame, and layd down their armes there, being a wet season. Some of whom continuing there the next day, A. W. went into the towne to see them. He knew some of their faces and they his; but he being a boy, and having no money, he could not then relieve them or make them drink; yet he talked with them about Oxford and his relations and acquaintance there; for the doing of which he was checked when he came home.'

The particulars of the Cavaliers' march out of Oxford were recorded by an eye-witness, whose de-scription of the affair was addressed to Speaker Lenthall and printed for the information of the public by the order of the House of Commons.

' On Wednesday the 24th of June says this special correspondent of the seventeenth century, ' the citizens surrendered The enemy marched out about twelve of the clock, being a very rainy day. A guard of our foot was appointed for them to march through, which extended in length from St. Clement's, near Maudlin Bridge, to Shotover Hill. The horse were drawn up into several bodies at other places. Those of the enemy who marched out in a body, well armed and with flying colours, and drums beating, were two thousand and upwards, besides officers, who received no injury in their. march through, nor the least affront; which the governor, Sir Thomas Glenham, hath since acknow-ledged, much for the honour of the army. The forerunners of those that marched forth, and the stragglers that came afterwards on the same day, being the most of them horsemen and private persons engaged in the seige, were near five hundred men. There likewise marched forth this day at the North Gate all those that went to Yorkshire and Gloucestershire, and those parts, who had a convoy for that purpose, being a considerable number. When Prince Rupert and Prince Maurice went forth on Monday, and those that followed on Tuesday, (when other men of quality left this city), there were in all about three hundred persons, most of them of good quality, since we came into the town. It hath been the continual employment of some, in the making of passes for those that were not left behind, and not marched out of the town with the body, there having been above two thousand passes made since we entered, of which there is a particular list of every man's name kept, there being many of them noble-men, knights, and gentlemen of quality, the rest officers, reformadoes, and some scholars. Likewise since we came into the town, the three regiments of auxiliaries, consisting of two thousand men, have been disbanded, and their names brought in. There are yet great numbers in that town, both officers, and soldiers, and strangers, that have not yet received their passea Those that marched out upon Wednesday, about nine hundred of them laid down their arms when they came to Thame, and received passes to go to their several houses, and their arms were brought into Oxford: one thousand and one hundred of them listed themselves for foreign service. We found in the Magazine seventy barrels of powder; besides they had two mills which supported them with powder. There were in the town thirty-eight pieces of ordnance, whereof twenty-six were brass. For provisions of victuals I cannot give you a particular account, only this is general, That by what we found in the stores, and by what we are informed they had in the store before they sold it to the towns-men, during the treaty, to raise moneys to pay their soldiers, there was not lesse than six moneths' provisions. The souldiers were much discontented, and much ado there was to preserve the lords whom they accused for being the occasion for de-livering up the town. For the strength of the works about the town, they are such, as I think any knowing man in martial affairs will say it was for your service the town was taken by conditions, especially considering what unseasonable weather hath followed: for, if we had continued the seige but to this day, we should have been forced to have quit some of the leaguers already made, the fields having been overflown with water. I have been with several of your 'acquaintance here in town, who were provided till Christmas with provisions, and do affirm that for corn, beef, salt, butter, and cheese, there was plenty for the said time: fresh meat for the great ones being the only thing complained of as a great want, and yet we found some store of that at the surrender. The general no sooner entered Oxford, but he called a council of war, and ordered his forces several wayes: four regiments to Worcester, two to Bagland, and two to Wallingford, which otherwise he could not have spared, had not the place been reduced : We may say truly, and you will so too, That it was a great mercy of God this place was so timously regained, considering what blood might have been spent about it, if the way of force had been taken: and more treasure it would have lost than the estates of those within would have satisfied.

'Sir,
' Your humble Servant.
' *Oxford,*
'JUNE 16th,1646.'

On the first day of the next month this narrative of the fall and evacuation of Oxford was printed and published by Edward Harland, at the order of the Commons.

CHAPTER VII

THE SAINTS TRIUMPHANT.

THOUGH the Oxonians of Elizabethan England and Stuart times learnt to regard royal visits with pride and gratulation, they continued to regard the inquisitions of imperial authority with suspicion and abhorrence, as dangerous and despotic interferences with their vested interests and rights of self-government. Each of the successive batches of royal visitors, who entered Oxford in the sixteenth century with powers to reform the university, accomplished work that was remembered by gownsmen with bitterness long after its doers had descended to the grave

But of all the visitors, appointed by supreme government to ascertain and correct academic abuses, none appeared so wicked and abominable to the scholars whom they ventured to punish, as those Parliamentarian inquisitors concerning whose doings Antony Wood remarks, 'Such cruelty was there showed, such tyranny acted by the clergy-visitors, and such alterations made by them, that never the like (no, not in those various times from King Henry VIII. to Queen Elizabeth) was ever seen or heard of. Many good wits were ejected, which, for want of improvement in any academical way, were soon quite lost and drowned. Others also lost that learning they had by seeking after a bare livelihood, or by suffering extreme misery either at home or in foreign countries, and all done for conscience-sake and the king, now a captive, and ready to receive the fatal blow from his subjects. But least these their sufferings should stand unrecorded to posterity, hundreds of silver and brass medals were made at the charges of some expelled, and dispersed into divers countries. On one side was the effigies of an altar, and this wrote on it, 'P. M. Acad. Oxon. 1648,' and on the reverse this, ' Deo, Ecclesirae, Principi, Victima.' At the same time also were the said words weaved in black ribbon with silver and gold letters, and commonly worn in hats by scholars and others: but so distasteful was it to Cheynell, that seeing a scholar going out of St. Mary's door before him (after sermon on Sunday) with a bunch of it tied in his hat, cocked, did with great fury snatch the hat from his head, pull it thence with disdain, tear or cut it in pieces and throw to the scholar his hat again.'

When Cheynell, one of the Puritan divines, com-missioned by the Parliament to labour for the conversion of Oxonian malignants, and one of the clerical visitors, on whose harshness Wood reflects, thus visited his wrath upon a wearer of the academical badge of loyalty, the scholars, who had sided with the vanquished king, were offering futile and irritating resistance to the emissaries of the *ipso facto* government, instead of conciliating them by such expressions of outward submission as they might have rendered without any ignominious sacrifice of principle to triumphant force.

That the loyal scholars are to be condemned for taking the only line of action which appeared to them compatible with fidelity to their sovereign, no generous observer of their imprudent conduct is likely at this date to suggest; but in fairness to the men, whose resentment they provoked, and whose severities they denounced, it must be borne in mind that the victims of the Parliamentary inquisition left nothing undone that was calculated to exasperate their adversaries and goad them into the adoption of a merciless policy.

If the 'beloved saints,' as the loyal Oxonians termed them derisively, were peremptory, overbearing, cruel, the gownsmen, ejected from their collegiate preferments by the authority of the 'blessed parliament were not innocent of studied insolence and undignified contumaciousness to their oppressors. Instead of meeting their enemies with manly resoluteness and proper courtesy, not a few of the Caroline doctors and their academic followers had recourse to paltry quibbles, petty evasions, and puerile impertinences in their vain attempts to bring the visitors to a stand-still. At the time, they were firmly convinced that their conduct would cover them with glory, and command the admiration of posterity; but no Englishmen of the present generation, capable of rightly appreciating their honourable motives, and properly commiserating their misfortunes, is unwilling to believe that, so soon as the blinding heats of contention had subsided, they reflected with dissatisfaction on many features of their opposition to the Parliamentarian commissioners. The ludicrous and painful scenes, which preceded and attended Mrs. Fell's forcible ejection from the deanery of Christ Church, are affairs on which it is impossible for any generous reader to reflect without regretful disapprobation of the resistance with whose general characteristics the lady's unfeminine and injurious stubbornness was in perfect harmony.

The disdainful answers of haughty dons, and the flippant contumacy of impudent students, stirred the resentment of the beloved saints, and strengthened them in their determination to purge the colleges of every principal, fellow, and undergraduate, who should decline to conform to the new order of things; and no one can deny the merit of thoroughness to the manner in which they accomplished their work, when after many hesitations and delays they proceeded to carry out the instructions of Parliament

When Philip Herbert, Earl of Pembroke—whom the Cavaliers ejected from the Chancellor's office in 1643, to make room for William Seymour, Marquis of Hertford—re-entered Oxford in the character of supreme governor of the university, he was attended by his "sons James and John, his grandson, the Earl of Carnarvon, a numerous retinue of gentlemen of high quality, and an imposing cavalcade of horsemen, who had ridden out from Oxford and met him at Abingdon. Troops accompanied him in such numbers that Wood, whilst ridiculing the pageant as contemptible, mean, and unworthy of an Oxford Chancellor, allows that the concourse of soldiers and civilians was mistaken for an 'army' by the country people between Abingdon and Oxford, who certainly would not have made such a blunder so soon after the civil war if the procession had been the insignificant gathering of country parsons, place-seekers, and officials which the Chancellor's detractors declared that it was. 'The visitors of the university went forth says Wood,' to meet the Chancellor as far as Abindon. Sir Nathaniel Brent, Dr. John Wilkinson of Magdalen Hall, Mr. Reynolds, and Mr. Corbet, rode in a coach together; Mr. Rogers and the other visitors, some heads of houses, the proctors elected by Parliament, a few country parsons who had brought their sons for fellowships, and divers scholars that were seekers after preferment, rode on hackney horses. When the whole company met at Abindon, there were above an hundred horsemen that drew themselves up in two divisions as wings to Pembroke's coach, in the spacious market-place there That the justices of Oxfordshire were not inadequately represented in the cavalcade the annalist reluctantly admits; and he further informs us that several hundreds of soldiers' of the Oxford garrison marched with colours flying and drums beating on either side of the procession through the streets of the town.

To bring derision on the Chancellor and his doings, the loyalist pamphleteers represented that he entered Oxford with such a beggarly crew of tatterdemalions as had never before attended a chief of the university on a public occasion. For instance, Tom Barlow, of Queen's College, in his ' Pegasus, or the Flying Horse from Oxford, bringing the proceedings of the Visitors, and other Bedlamites there, by the command of the Earl of Montgomery giving a satirical account of the affair, wrote, ' Tuesday, April the 11th, the long-legged piece of impertinency (which they miscall Chancellor) was to be brought with state into Oxon. To this end these few inconsiderable and ill-faced saints hired all the hackneys in the town (which were basely bad, yet good enough for them). Out they went and met the Hoghen-Moghen, I told you of. What courtship passed between them at meeting, how he swore at them, and they said grace at him; how many zealous faces and ill legs they made, and at what distance I know not: a long time they made about it At last they came, and the governor and his regiment meets them at Fryer Bacon's study, where you might have seen the Presbyterian and Independent agreed against the poor Christians of Oxon. In the mean time Thomas Smith, of Magdalen College, had an excellent design; and that he might have suitable accommodation, would needs borrow an ass; nay, an ass he would have and ride in next the Chancellor; and when they told him it was a mad trick, he told them no, for he knew there would be many asses besides his. And now they came! they came! And indeed it was such a miserable pageant as I never saw. Had you seen tall Pembroke in the midst of those little inspired Levites, you would have sworn you had seen Saul once more among the prophets. Along they came, without any respect from those in the streets (which were not many); not a cap or knee from them, but frowns and curses; and 'twas a wonder but that the soldiers guarded them that they had not welcomed them with old eggs and apples. Aaron Rogers, Langley, and squint-eyed Greenwood, were the chief men (what the worst were, when those were the best, you may judge), and with them about ten or twelve scholars more, fresh-men and all, only they were interlarded with some country parsons who brought their sons for fellowships, and so worshipped the beast for profit.'

Though Thomas Barlow worded his narrative so as to imply that the Chancellor's procession was headed by the malapert member of Magdalen College, riding the animal whose meanness and stubbornness and perversity were supposed to be typical of the Parliamentarian government, it is almost needless to remark that Mr. Thomas Smith was not permitted to make himself ridiculous in order to draw derision on the chief of the university. The scribe's malice, however, had the desired effect on the Cavaliers of the country, who found momentary consolation for their urgent sorrows, in applauding the scholars, whose excellent design had caused the Oxonian populace to receive the long-legged Pembroke with appropriate contempt.

Nor was Mr. Smith's asinine scheme the only project for showing the chancellor in what contempt he was held by the loyal scholars. A waggish gentleman of the university had prepared for delivery in South Street (as it was then called),—' at Christ Church Gate, against Pembroke College where a strong body of Puritan students had resolved to receive their chancellor — the following ironical speech: ' My Lord, you are surrounded, and lest you should be tired with civilities between Christ Church and Pembroke, I shall be plain and brief Sir, without preface or ceremony, you are welcome to us; the genius of the place salutes you, chancellor; the severest muses smooth their brows; and all the graces begin to smile. Muses and Graces cry, "Welcome, Pembroke!" Hark! how your college sounds; the scholars learn of the buildings to echo forth your praise and welcome. Hark! how it rings again! Thrice welcome, noble chancellor; welcome, Pembroke!' The mockery of this reference to the comparative emptiness and silence of Pembroke, which had distinguished itself amongst the loyal houses by enthusiasm for the royal cause, notwithstanding its association with the name and family of the Parliamentarian chancellor, would, it was hoped, raise the laughter of the bystanders and put the appointed orator of the Puritans so completely out of countenance, that he would not remember a word of the sanctimonious speech which it would devolve upon him to deliver, in praise of the earl and the rebellious parliament. Should the irony of the mock-address escape detection, the mischievous students were prepared to turn to account the cheers elicited by their misinterpreted impudence, and to put their intentions beyond the possibility of misapprehension by a still more absurd oration, which another of their party had promised to utter so soon as the applause of the 'well-affected' auditors should die out.

The second speech prepared for the annoyance of the chancellor, whose attachment to saintly men and ways had neither corrected his constitutional irritability nor amended his habit of swearing impiously during his frequent paroxysms of rage, was composed of the following words: —' My Lord, I am, as your honour is, in haste, and therefore shall not be so uncivil as to detain you longer with civilities. I perceive the youths begin to kindle through all in love, yet love and joy when youths are overjoyed, are rude and boisterous. See how their caps begin to fly, and seriously but that they mean to run bare-headed whilst you are here, they would even throw away their very heads and leggs. See, yonder is an arm for joy thrown out of joint; that legg is even displaced; 'twill scarce ever find the way back to the body; but we must change our phrase and garb, and now give way to them whose prudence and gravity hath called them to present businesses of higher concernment to your saddest thoughts.

But though the conspirators against the chancellor's peace of mind had laid their plans with considerable cleverness, and had exercised commendable forethought in providing themselves with a second oratorical piece for use in case the first should miss fire, they were disappointed in their hope of creating a ludicrous misadventure for the earl and the 'well-affected youths in the space between the great gate of Christ Church and the approach to Pembroke College. Shortly before the plot should have succeeded, a heavy fall of rain rescued the chancellor from the enemies who were lying in wait to destroy his mental composure. This untimely shower, which began shortly after the earl had quitted his coach for the back of a splendid charger, decided the leaders of the cavalcade to push on past Christ Church and drop from the ceremonious proceedings the pre-arranged address of the evangelical students. The conspirators, therefore, endured the mortification of seeing the odious chancellor, strongly guarded by the governor's troops, ride bravely onwards to Quatervois, where the mis-creant Cheynell demonstrated the degradation of the schools, and won the applause of the Latinless rabble, by receiving the supreme governor of the university — with an English oration. Poor Anto-nius à Bosco speaks with natural bitterness of ' the cursed shower and soldiers that together prevented the 'wags' (Antony spells it with a second g) from throwing their squibs at the long-legged earl; but it is probable that, in spite of the storm, the chancellor would have pulled rein at Christ Church gate, and his guard would have allowed the assembled scholars to approach his person, had he not been forewarned of the hostile and mutinous intentions of the wags.

Nor were the malcontent gownsmen long in discovering that the visitors and chancellor, backed by rebels of Westminster, were not to be driven from their purposes by jests and scornful words. The work of 'reformation' went on briskly. Every week witnessed an increase in the number of godly tutors and pious schoolboys, who flocked to the university to get possession of the fellowships and scholarships, rendered vacant by the expulsion of Charles Stuart's malignant adherents. It was of no avail to himself or his party that Robert Whitehall replied to the visitor's summons, 'As I am summoned a student of Christ's Church, my name itself speaks for me, that I can acknowledge no visitation but King Charles.

My name's Whitehall, God bless the Poet,
If I submit, the King shall know it

Mr. John Carrick, of the same college, merely cut his own academic throat, when, in mockery of Puritanical phraseology, he wrote, 'I profess unto you I will not submit to the visitation ; yea, verily I say unto you I will not submit' The jesters lost the game, and when the excitement of contumacy was over they found small occasion for hilarity in the result of their transactions with the saintly visitors.

If it were my object to mix a cup that should tickle the palates of a single section of Oxonians, and prove ungrateful to a more numerous and thoughtful body of Alma Mater's children, I should at this point throw into my text some bitter reflections on the men who, whilst driving from the university several unscrupulous agitators, whose expulsion from their colleges was requisite for the well-being of the academic community and the entire state, reduced to poverty a number of learned and excellent gentlemen, whose only fault was their justifiable devotion to a vanquished cause. But there is no need to add to the reproaches which almost countless writers and speakers have cast upon the Parliamentarian visitors, whose patriotism and honesty were not inferior to the public spirit and sincerity of the general run of their opponents, On the contrary, the Parliamentarian reformers of Oxford have been so egregiously slandered by reckless distributors of invective that an Englishman's love of justice and fair play would incline me at any suitable opportunity to speak favourably of their motives, and vindicate their reputations from the charges of deliberate brutality and sordid lust of gain, which have been preferred against them. Upon the whole they were what they declared, and believed themselves to be, devout and benevolent men, earnestly desirous to promote righteousness and increase the not superabundant happiness of their fellow-creatures. But though I take this view of their aims and doings, I am not surprised that the Royalist scholars judged them very differently. Moreover, it would not take much to draw from me an admission that some of the most conscientious of these terrible commissioners discharged their invidious functions in an indescribably offensive manner.

Good men, even in these days of fine breeding and universal considerateness, are sometimes no less disagreeable than virtuous. And I doubt not that the Puritan inquisitors were at no pains to soothe the indignation of the scornful doctors and supercilious dons, who told them they were so many illiterate and hypocritical thieves. I doubt not that even when they forbore to repay contumely with abuse, there was something in the mild intonations of their whining voices, and in the quiet resoluteness of their lugubrious faces, which said very distinctly, 'Gentlemen, when you were above us, you made us feel it; and now that we have got you under our feet, we mean to let you know it.'

The list of expulsed scholars was a long one, and the names of the proscribed students were exhibited on the walls of the various colleges, together with notices to the effect that the gentlemen so distinguished would consider themselves expelled, and retire peacefully to the country, or prepare to make personal acquaintance with the sharpest rigour of military discipline. And when the condemned gownsmen, carrying their policy of resistance even to the verge of rebellion against the existing government, not only lingered in the university from which they had been ordered to withdraw, but had the hardihood to seek conflicts with the soldiers of the garrison, a serjeant, with a guard of musketeers and a drummer, went to every college and hall within Alma Mater's bounds, and with all proper drumming, and halting, and shouldering of a-r-r-ms, published the following order, issued by the deputy-governor of the city, Thomas Keylsey.

'Whereas I have received orders from his excel-lency the Lord Fairfax to cause all orders of Parliament for the reformation of this place to be put in execution, and have, in order thereunto, received a special order from the Committee of Lords and Commons for the reformation of this university, for the expulsion of divers gentle-men, whose names have been publicly affixed, that they might have notice to pro-vide for their removal, and since that time divers affronts have been offered .to the soldiery of this garrison, as fyering at the guard, and causing alarums in the city, and not knowing of what evil consequence it may be to suffer such disaffected persons in the garrison, I am constrained to hasten the execution of the orders aforesaid, and do therefore hereby require all and every of the gentlemen, whose names have been publickly affixed, to depart from the garrison this very day, and in case any shall refuse to remove, I shall after this day take him for a spie and deal with him accordingly. Given under my hand at Oxon, this 5 of July, 1648.—THO. KEYLSEY."

To treat this notice with an affectation of disregard for the source whence it emanated would have been sheer madness. The scholars, who would gladly have shed their blood for their king in a field of battle, had no ambition to be led forth, hands tied and eyes blinded, and be shot into an open pit by a file of Roundhead musketeers. Still farther were they from a wish to be hung by their necks on gibbets fixed against their colleges. The order had the desired effect on the batches of expelled gownsmen against whom it was directed, though it was found necessary to repeat it for the benefit of other lots of condemned academicians.

A few of the more obstinate and fool-hardy of the ejected scholars had indeed the temerity to tarry in Oxford after the publication of the order, which rendered them liable to be dealt with as spies, and even to concern themselves in an absurd plot for bringing the Oxford garrison over to the side of the utterly beaten and discredited Cavaliers. Some of these maniacal gentlemen fell into the hands of Deputy-Governor Keylsey, who, forbearing to put his threat into execution, was content to cure their illusions, and teach them submissiveness by the diet and close confinement of prison discipline. But the menace put an end to the scholars' schemes for unanimously resisting the sentences of the Visitors. The Royalist tutors moved off to the country, car-' rying with them batches of Cavalier undergraduates, who pursued their studies for the next few months, in some cases for years, in the provincial towns and rural villages, where their teachers opened schools for the instruction of the sons of the neighbouring Royalist gentry. Other gownsmen, implicated in the attempt to create a mutiny amongst the troops, fled precipitately to places of concealment, or to ports where they embarked for Ireland or the Continent. Mr. Thomas Smith, of Magdalen, saddled his donkey, and rode away to his native shire; and Bob Whitehall, the 'time-serving and pot-poet of Christ Church as Wood terms him, retreated to a scene of rustic tranquillity, where reflective and dispassionate consideration of the state of public affairs, and his private interests, wrought such a change in his temper and principles that, in spite of his brave words, he was glad to eat humble pie before the Visitors, and through Richard Ingoldsby's influence obtain a place on the foundation of Merton College.

In the following year Thomas, Lord Fairfax, still at the height of his popularity, though his influence was rapidly yielding to the growing power of the future protector of the Commonwealth, entered Oxford in state, May 17, 1649, together with Cromwell, Sir Hardress Waller, Thomas Harrison, Richard Ingoldsby, (Governor of Oxford,) John Hewson, John Okey, Edward Grosvenor, Owen Rowe, William Goffe, and other military personages, who were naturally desirous to see the good results of the latest reformation of Oxford. Great was the excitement occasioned by the arrival of these martial chiefs in the city of learning, and the pomp of their reception was not inferior to the ostentatious ceremony with which the scholars of former times had welcomed royal visitors to their pleasant places. Fairfax and Cromwell lodged at All Souls' College, but they honoured Magdalen College by appearing at a mid-day dinner which the members of that house provided for King Charles's conquerors. On rising from table Fairfax, Cromwell, and their military comrades, withdrew from the Common Hall of their entertainers to the bowling-green, where they played bowls with abundant spirit and dexterity till it was time for them to proceed to the Convocation House, where the general of all the forces in England and Ireland, and the future protector of the state were made Doctors of Civil Law, and their less august associates were invested with the robes and privileges of Masters of Arts.

Eight months later, Oliver Cromwell had succeeded Philip, Earl of Pembroke, in the Chancellorship of Oxford University, which office after Oliver's death was filled by his son, the Protector Richard.

CHAPTER VII

CROMWELLIAN OXFORD.

WHILST the Parliamentarian reformers were purg-ing Oxford of malignant8, one of the wittiest and most scholarly of the Oxonian Cavaliers,—Dr. John Allibond, Vicar of Bradwell, Gloucestershire, and formerly master of the free school adjoining Magdalen College, of which society he was a member,— exhibited the 'blessed saints' to derision in his ' Rustica Descriptio Visitationis Fanaticae,' a ballad composed in Macaronic Latin, of which the following verses are a specimen :—

' Rumore nuper est delatum,
Dum agebamus ruri,
Oxonium iri reformatum,
Ab iis qui dicti Puri.

' Decrevi itaque confestim,
(Obstaculis sublatis) Me oculatum dare testem Hujusce novitatis.

' Ingressus urbem juxta morem,
Scrulandi desiderio:
Nil praeter maciem et squalorem
Fedissimum comperio.

' A Decio in specum jacti,
Qui tantum dormierunt,
Post saeculum expergefacti,
Tot mira non viderunt.

' Erectas illi crebras cruces,
Et Templa conspexere,
Quæ prisci pietatis duces '
Tunc primum construxere.

' Nos autem sanctiora nuper
Incidimus in saecula,
Qui tollunt ista, tanquam super-
Stitionis symbola.

' Ad Scholas primum me trahebat
Comitiorum norma,
Queis olim quisque peragebat
Solenniter pro forma.

' Expecto Eegis Professores,
Comparuere nulli:
Nee illinc addunt Inceptores,
Nec togae, nec cuculli.

' Calcavi atrium quadratum,
Quo juvenum examen
Confluxit olim : video pratum
Quod densum tegit gramen.

' Adibam lubens scholam Musices,
Quam feminae et joci
Ornassent pridem, sed tibicines
Jam nusquam erant loci.

' Conscendo orbis illud decus,
Bodleio fundatore;
Sed intus erat nullum pecus,
Excepto janitore.

'Neglectos vidi libros multos,
Quod minime mirandum:
Nam inter bardos tot et stultos
There's few could understand 'em.'

In spite of orders prohibiting the publication of pasquinades and pamphlets written in derision of the visitors, Dr. Allibond's ' Rustica Descriptio' was twice printed in .1648, and was circulated no less widely in manuscript than in type. Dons and undergraduates bought with avidity the single sheet on which the classic doggrel was printed; and in order that the production might afford amusement to a larger public, incapable of construing for themselves the Macaronic Latin, of which there were two hundred and four lines, the author, after a while, published the following English version of his witty performance, preluded with an announcement that the translation was put forth not for the ladies, but for the members of the unlearned Parliament,—' in usum reformatae donms parliamenti, sive parliament! indoctorum, ejusdem nominis secundi—

' I learned by intelligence sure,
As I lived in my rural retreat,
That reformers, snrnamed the
Pure, "Were remodelling science's seat.

' So I hastened to saddle my steed,
And onwards to Oxford I trotted,
To see what was done or decreed
By reformers so very besotted.

' I entered the Muses' abode,
And sought for my friends, as of yore;
Nothing else could I see, as I rode,
But filth, want, and woe at each door.

'Sure never since Decius's days,
"Were changes beheld such as those,—
When the Sleepers (as history says)
Started up from their hundred years' doze.
'And saw Christian churches around,
Towers, crosses uprear'd to the skies,
Pagan idols and altars thrown down,
But scarcely could credit their eyes.

' My wonder, though similar, springs
From changes the very reverse,
They have voted our churches foul things,
And destroy'd them or chang'd them for worse.

Impatient I fly to the schools,
Where logic once sat on her throne,
For I wanted to see what the rules
Of reforming committees had done.

' I look'd for Inceptors in vain,
No Royal Professors were there,
And I saw that the Puritan train
Neither caps, gowns, nor tippets would wear

'Through the schools deeply musing I pass,
All was solitude, silence, disgrace;
The square was all covered with grass,
For few ever came to the place.

' Next I bent my sad steps to the floor,
Where music was wont to invite;
No performers were ranged on the floor,
Loves and Graces had taken their flight.

' Next I crawled to the building of Bodley,
That glory and grace of our isle;
None was there but the porter—the
Godly Had rather be distant a mile.

' The books they lay scattered around;
Few opened, and still fewer scann'd 'em,

For dunces increase and abound,
And Puritans can't understand 'em.

' Next day, being Sunday, I went,
To service and sermon at Mary's;
For she is no longer a saint,
In the bede-roll of Typping and Harrys.

' I fear'd that I should not obtain
Room for sitting or standing within ;
But I found that my fears were all vain,
For the meeting was scanty and thin.

'As a senior, I boldly proceed
To the seats which to seniors belong;
But tailors, cooks, scullions, impede,
A base and unmannerly throng.

' The Vice-Chancellor, recently made,
Marches forth,—he has learning enough,
But too little conscience, 'tis said,
Being formed of most flexible stuff.

' No keys had the Proctors to show,
As badges of honour and trust;
No staves had the Bedels—
I trow Some with laughter were ready to burst.

'A vain, vapid preacher, or Fungus,
The pulpit ascended—the fellow
Was known for a dull man among us,
But began to thump cushion, and bellow

'Whatever came into his mouth,
He was ready to pour forth and spout,
With clench'd fist and action uncouth,—
But the orator never was out

'Sick and weary with trash without end,
I could not have patience to stay;
'So back'd out to visit a friend,
If friends were not all chased away.

'First to All Souls I went in my round,
The name suits the state of the College,
Few bodies were there to be found,
And those were without *VOVC* or knowledge.

'I asked for the Warden, and sigh'd,
A man by each virtue adorn'd,
"In ward is the warden," they cried,
But the scoff and the scoffers I scorn'd.

'Hence to Corpus I hastened, and saw
Its dignity turn'd to disgrace;
The governor rul'd without law,
Its learning had fled from the place.

'How is Christ Church subverted and tost,
Like a ship, in its ocean of woe!
And where is its talented host?
All are outcasts and wanderers now.

'Where the Orator Public, whose mind,
Like his voice, was our pride and delight?
In a dungeon the saint is confin'd,

And good men grow sick at the sight.

' To St. John's I directed my course,
To see its condition I dreaded,
Its fate was like John's—something worse—
For twice was the college beheaded.

 When the Rebels took off the last head,
Young and old men resolved to retreat,
A daemon now rules in his stead,
And there's nothing to drink—or to eat.

' Fair mansion ! thy rivulets ran,
And pleasantly watered the ground ;
Now Channel, a monster, no man,
Spreads his filth and corruption around.

' Though Trinity College was near,
I had not the heart to go in;
It has become tainted, I hear,
By a sort of heretical sin.

' Desolation has spread its domain
Through garden, and chapel, and square;
No scholars or fellows remain,
No Hannibal Potter is there!

' The College with Nozle of Brass,
I visit upon my return; Sad news did
I hear as I pass,
And hearing, I could not but mourn.

'The Reformers, by force or by art,

Have a wretch for its Principal nam'd;
Of whose crooked eye-sight and heart
Dame Nature is sick and asham'd.

' I next seek the College, whose years
Have produc'd no effect on its name;
That name is still New—what my fears
When near to the building I came.
'I heard wretched wailings and woes,
In a house to the Muses so dear;
From torture these shriekings arose,—
The Puritans kept their racks here

' Next Magdalen weeping extends
Her empty enclosures to me;
I wept, when no fellows, no friends,
Where nought but a desert I

' She lately could number a race
Of high-minded youth, her Demies,
Her pillars were strong, and the place
Was upheld by the holy and wise.

'Those props and those pillars are gone,
And prostrate she lies on the ground,
Depriv'd of her children, forlorn,
She mourns o'er her losses around.

' The Muses were wont to repair
To her realms of religion and peace;
Now dullness and darkness are there,
And all sorts of monsters increase.

' For President, Goodwin presides,
A dunce, dismal, doleful, and dull;
So queer is his head-dress besides,
That nine caps adorn the numskull.

' Ah, Oxford! that fate I deplore;
I fear lest the spirits accurst
Have return'd, which were cast out of yore,
And brought others worse than the first.

' Wherever my footsteps I bent,
On whatever I fasten'd my eye,
Now sorrow, and now merriment,
Excited the laugh or the cry.

' I wept o'er the wise, learned, and good,
From groves academic ejected;
I laugh'd at the dismal dull brood,
The elect, in their places elected.

' Reform is a very fine art,
'Tis a med'cine most rapid and sure,
'Tis a knife to cut off the sick part,
But more likely to kill than to cure.

' It bids us pluck up root and branch
Those in principle rooted and grounded;
It makes caps square, and men square, and staunch,
Give place to the rogue and the Roundhead.

' If you ask for the colleges, they
Point to walls and to towers with a grin;
Nothing else can you see, if you stay,

For no scholars are dwelling within.

' Cold as frost are the stoves and the grates,
Chapels silent as graves, and the hall
Never hears sounds of trenchers and plates;
In the cellars no beer strong or small.

'If to churches you wish to repair,
Something sacred to hear and to
There's nothing but quackery there,
But stammering *extempore,*

' And how do the citizens fare,
With all their reforming devices,
Who help'd us to what we now are,
And courted this terrible crisis.

' You proudly exalted your horn,
When the mountain was groaning within er ;
But what you once hoped for you scorn,
And bravely you fere without dinner.

' The glory wert thou of our land,
Oh, Oxford! and honoured thy name;
How is it (I can't understand)
Though the same, that thou art not the same ?

' What dreamer in visions of night,
Ever fancied what's happen'd to me ?
All distorted, reversed to my sight,
And no Oxford in Oxford I see.'

Whilst the Cavaliers of the various counties, repeating the contradictory assertions of the 'Rustica Descriptio,' alternately bewailed the desolation of Oxford, where grass was said to have overgrown the schools' quadrangle, and inveighed against the lugubrious characteristics of the Puritan scholars, who occupied the tenantless colleges, students flocked to Alma Mater in such numbers, that in 1651 the registered members of the university exceeded by nearly four hundred the matriculated population of the year 1622. But there is no need to repeat the facts stated in an earlier chapter of this work to demonstrate that, compared with the period between the commencement of the Civil War and Charles the First's execution, the interval between that King's death and his son's restoration was a time of academic revival, which saw a steady growth in the populousness of the seat of learning and several important additions to its wealth. During the years of scholastic disturbance and Puritan ascendency, —*i.e.* between the Cavalier occupation of Oxford and the revival of the Episcopacy—Alma Mater and her colleges acquired several important benefactions, such as the Craven University scholarships, the Radcliffe and Milward scholarships of Brasenose, the Gwynne scholarships of Jesus, the Goodridge scholarships of Wadham, and the Rouse scholarships of Pembroke.

Nor may it be imagined that the Cavaliers were excluded from Oxford throughout the long continu-ance of the Puritan triumph. As soon as the Visitation had rearranged the university in accordance with the views of the dominant party of the State, the Cavalier gownsmen were permitted to return to the colleges, and to pursue their studies in their old haunts so long as they conformed outwardly to the new regulations, and forebore from acting in open defiance of existing authorities. Coffeehouses came into fashion at Oxford during the Commonwealth; and though the coffee-room patronized by the King's friends was known to be a political club, where the adherents of the banished Stuarts assembled to gossip rancorously about the iniquities of the Usurper's Government, the despot, who was at the same time Protector of the Republic and Chancellor of the University, took no steps for its suppression. 'In this year (1655),' says Antony Wood, ' Arth. Tillyard, apothecary and great Royalist, sold coffee publicly in his house against All Souls' Coll. He was encouraged so to do by some Royalists, now living in Oxon, and by others, who esteemed themselves either virtuosi or wits; of which the chiefest number were of All Souls' Coll' The Protector-Chancellor was too prudent to see what it was his interest not to recognize; and in other matters, not less menacing to his government, he allowed considerable licence to the gownsmen who were amongst his bitterest and most unscrupulous adversaries. Whilst the use of the Common Prayer was prohibited even in private houses, and the canonical vestments of the episcopal clergy were deemed profane and superstitious rags, it was known that Royalist gownsmen in orders persisted in the secret use of the proscribed offices, and were accustomed to perform the services of the Anglican liturgy to secret congregations of fellow-churchmen, in exact accordance with rubrical requirements. And instead of bestirring himself to expose and punish these offenders against discipline, as some fifteen or twenty years earlier Laud hunted down and chastised the frequenters of secret conventicles, Cromwell was well content that they should disregard the law in private, so long as they observed it in public.

At the same time the general appearance of the academic residents was notably devoid of the doleful severity and austere sadness which, according to the humorous misrepresentations of Cavalier wits, dis-tinguished the gownsmen of the Puritan regime. On the contrary, the Visitors had scarcely put their friends in the offices of the ejected Royalists, when they found it necessary to ' reform Reformation as Wood expresses it, and exert themselves to restrain the younger and more frivolous members of the university from indulging in vain pursuits and carnal pleasures, expressly prohibited by the Caroline Code.

' The next matter says Wood, under date 1650, 'was that all scholars should in their manners and habit conform themselves to the statutes of the university, and also that they forbear " all excess and vanity in powdering their hair, wearing knots of ribands " on their clothes and in their hats, " walking in boots, spurs, and boot-hose-tops." That none also keep hounds or horses (now a common practice, yet not usual among scholars here-to-fore), but follow those studies required by their respective statutes. These vanities being common, some governors and many preachers were guilty of them, and went more like persons of the inns of court or playhouses, rather than such that were to deliver the oracles of God. Instead of short hair, collar-band with cassock, in a pulpit, you might have beheld long powdered hair, large bands and half-shirts hanging out at their sleeves, and they themselves accounting nothing more ridiculous than starcht formality of a prelati-cal cut. As for caps, either round or square, none were worn publicly, only in some colleges at refection or scholastical exercise.' Whence it appears that, instead of rendering the students more precise, formal, and sad, the Puritan reformation was clearly a period in which the scholars were remarkable for foppishness, gaiety, and addiction to expensive pleasures.

John Evelyn the diarist, having in early life received a part of his scholastic training at Balliol College, paid Oxford several visits in the subsequent stages of his career; and in July, 1654, he and his wife made a trip to the university, when he witnessed the celebration of the Act in St Mary's Church, and saw the Puritan innovators rendering due respect to the ancient usages and traditions of the schools in all matters not pertaining strictly to religion. On the eve of the Act (July 6th) the travellers arrived at Oxford, where they spent the next day ' in hearing several exercises in the schools and witnessing the ceremony of opening the Act 'After dinner,' says the diarist, 'the proctor opened the Act at St Mary's (according to custom), and the prevaricators their drollery, The doctors disputed We supped at Wadham.' The diarist's account of the next two days runs thus: ' 9th. Dr. French preached at St. Mary's on Matt. xii. 42, advising the students to search after true wisdom, not to be had in the books of philosophers; but in the Scriptures alone. In the afternoon, the famous Independent, Dr. Owen, perstringeing Episcopacy. He was now Cromwell's Vice-Chancellor. We dined with Dr. Ward, mathematical professor (since Bishop of Sarum), and at night supped in Balliol College Hall, where I had once been student and fellow-commoner, and where they made me extraordinarily welcome. 10th. On Monday, I went again to the schools, to hear several faculties, and in the afternoon tarried out the whole Act in St. Mary's, the long speeches of the proctors, the vice-chancellor, the several professors, creation of doctors, by the cap, ring, and kiss, &c., those ancient ceremonies and institutions being as yet not wholly abolished. Dr. Kendal, now Inceptor amongst others, performing his Act incomparably well, concluding it with an excellent oration, abating his Presbyterian animosities, which he withheld, not even against that learned and pious divine, Dr. Hammond. The Act was closed with the speech of the vice-chancellor, there being but four in theology and three in medicine, which was thought a considerable matter, the times considered. I dined at one Monsieur Fiat's, a student of Exeter College, and supped at a magnificent entertainment of Wadham Hall, invited by my dear and excellent friend, Dr. Wilkins, then Warden (after, Bishop of Chester).'

On the next day (Tuesday, the 11th day of July), Mr. and Mrs. Evelyn went to a musical entertainment at All Souls, paid a visit to 'that miracle of a youth, Mr. Christopher Wren,' called on Mr. Barlow, the librarian of the Bodleian galleries, and visited the Convocation House, Divinity School, and Physic School. Wednesday saw them at St. John's, New, Magdalen, And ' the Physic garden, where says the diarist, ' the sensitive plant was showed us for a great wonder.' Their doings on the next and last day of their visit are recorded thus: '13th. We all dined at that most obliging and universally curious Dr. Wilkins's, at Wadham College. He was the first who showed me the transparent apiaries, which he had built like castles and palaces, and so ordered them one upon another, as to take the honey without destroying the bees. These were adorned with a variety of dials, little statues, vanes, &c., and he was so abundantly civil, finding me pleased with them, to present me with one of the hives which he had empty, and which I afterwards had in my garden at Saye's Court, where it continued many years, and which his Majesty came on purpose to see and contemplate with such satisfaction. He had also contrived a hollow statue, which gave a voice and uttered words by a long concealed pipe that went to its mouth, whilst one speaks through it at a good distance. He had, above in his lodgings and gallery, a variety of shadows, dials, perspectives, and many other artificial, mathematical, and magical curiosities, a way-wiser, a thermometer, a monstrous magnet, conic and other sections, a balance on a semicircle; most of them of his own, and that prodigious young scholar, Mr. Christopher Wren; who presented me with a piece of white marble, which he had stained with a lively red, very deep, as beautiful as if it had been natural.'

The courtesies and hospitable civilities, lavished on Mr. and Mrs. Evelyn on this occasion, indicate that the Oxonians of the Commonwealth period were not wanting in affability and considerateness to their guests who flocked to Alma Mater for the festivities and diversion of Act Week — the equivalent of our modern Commemoration Week. That those same Oxonians were chargeable neither with indolence nor with want of success in their studies we know from the testimony of the Royalist partisan, Clarendon, who, after calling the Puritan visitation a ' wild and barbarous depopulation and reflecting on the enormous amount of stupidity and ignorance' which the visitors threw into Oxford, reluctantly admits that by God's blessing Alma Mater's generous and virtuous soil so changed the quality of the seed thus sown in her scholastic grounds, that, instead of producing an unprecedented crop of ignorance, profanation, atheism, and rebellion,' it yielded an abundance of piety and wisdom. 'When,' says the Cavalier historian, 'it pleased God to bring King Charles II. back to the throne, he found that university (not to undervalue the other, which had nobly likewise rejected the ill infusions which had been industriously poured into it) abounding in excellent learning, and devoted to duty and obedience, little inferior to what it was before its desolation.'

CHAPTER IX.

ALMA MATER IN THE DAYS OF THE MERRY MONARCH.

TIME and the various sufferings, consequent on a revolution which reduced a considerable proportion of them from affluence to grinding penury, had grievously thinned the ranks of the ejected Cavaliers, before the Restoration recalled the survivors to their academic offices, and put Puritanism once again under the foot of Episcopacy. But though bereaved of a large number of their companions in adversity, Royalist gownsmen, who had lost their preferments from decisions of Parliamentarian visitors, were an important element in the social force that' welcomed the Stuarts from exile, and enabled the reactionary politicians to nullify most of the reforms which had been effected during the interregnum.

They were the first and loudest in urging upon the advisers of the monarch that justice should restore all things,—the peers to their senatorial chamber, the confiscated lands to ecclesiastical corporations, Latin to the records, French to the law-courts, common prayer to the churches, bishops to the sees, archbishops to the provinces, splendour to the court, life and wit to the theatres, and place men of all degrees, laical or clerical, to the places from which democratic violence had driven them. Nor was the Stuart slow to grant their petition. The crisis brought to his palace an army of gentle mendicants,—men who after beggaring themselves in his father's service had shared the hardships and humiliations of exile; others who, though they had lived on their encumbered estates from the martyr's death to his son's return, had never ceased to plot and pray for the Restoration, or failed to contribute from their straitened means pecuniary aid to distressed Cavaliers; and a yet larger body of far more importunate beggars, who, on the revival of the dynasty which they had neither spent a coin nor spoken a word to reanimate, demanded recompense for all the services which they imagined themselves to have rendered to the royal . cause.

Gratitude and prudence required that something should be done to satisfy the more deserving or more influential of these applicants. The King, who was not so utterly devoid of generosity and honour as his enemies maintain, desired to relieve many of the suitors out of regard for their devotion and conspicuous services to his house. Others, though the lukewarmness of their loyalty and the selfishness of their action in past time were not unknown to him, he was constrained to treat as though he believed all their impudent assertions of fidelity to his throne, because they were so powerful, that to disappoint their cupidity might convert them from useful, though time-serving, supporters, to dangerous enemiea But without measures of spoliation it was impossible for the sovereign to satisfy or soothe a sufficient number of these hungry and vociferous claimants, who required more substantial proofs of their prince's regard than pleasant speeches and invitations to his galleries. Moreover, a policy of retaliation commended itself to the imperfect notions of justice generally prevalent amongst our ancestors of the seventeenth century.

So soon as he had felt his way with public opinion and ascertained his strength, Charles determined to reward his adherents and conciliate his insincere but powerful supporters, with spoils taken from men who had participated in the Puritan rebellion, or, if they had not been actually guilty of open disaffection to his cause, were known to favour opinions supposed to be hostile to monarchy and episcopacy. In accordance with this determination—which appeared altogether just to Royalists, and not altogether unjust to their opponents—royal visitors were appointed in the June of 1660, to accomplish a new reformation at Oxford, and do unto the Puritans of the schools even as the Parliamentarian visitors had in former time done unto the Royalist gownsmen.

A rush was made to Alma Mater's ground by the Caroline doctors and tutors, who, in the language of indignation and bitter resentment, told the King's commissioners with what contumely and flagrant cruelty they had been abused and beggared by the emissaries of the rebel parliament Nor had they any reason to complain of incredulity or neglect on the part of the tribunal to which they told their wrongs. In addition to restorations statutably or irregularly effected in various colleges, before the appointment of the commission, several Oxonian principals were speedily restored to the houses which they had governed in days prior to the triumph of the saints. Dr. Thomas Walker re-entered the lodge of University College; Dr. Gilbert Sheldon, without the intervention of the .Visitors, and indeed before they had official existence, regained the wardenship of All Souls—a place which he soon vacated on his promotion to the bishopric of London; Thomas Goodwyn was turned out of his pleasant quarters in Magdalen College, in order that Dr. John Oliver might again rule William of Waynfleet's house; Dr. Thomas Yate recovered the principal-ship of Brasenose, and was. not slow to put outside the college-gate the malapert Daniel Greenwood, who in the days of Puritan insolency had ventured to deride Thomas Yate's election to the principal's office as ' mere foppery;' at Corpus Dr. Edmund Staunton was ejected in favour of Dr. Robert Newlin, restored in the name of justice; at Christ Church Drs. Edward Reynolds, George Morley, and John Fell attained in quick succession the office from which the Puritan John Owen had been ' outed' so early as the end of 1659; and though the famous Mrs. Fell never returned to Christ Church in her husband's life, she lived to carry out in her son's time her threat of walking on her legs into the deanery from which she was removed by force; Trinity welcomed once again her beloved Hannibal Potter; Dr. Richard Baylis, whose initials on some of the money minted at New Inn commemorate his pecuniary services to Charles the First, was restored to the headship of St. John's College; Dr. Francis

Mansell again found himself principal of Jesus; at Pembroke Henry Wightwick recovered the mastership, from which he was subsequently 'ejected for scandalous behaviour.' And whilst these Oxonian principals were receiving the congratulations of society on their recovery of offices from which they had been driven by hypocritical usurpers, the Royal Visitors were restoring scores of fellows to the less exalted preferments which they had lost through the same revolution.

Recalling the agreeable incidents of this academic reformation, and other results of the king's return, Antony Wood observes: ' The scene of all things is now changed, and alterations made in the countenances, actions, manners, and words of all men. Those that for these twelve years last past had governed and carried all things in a manner at their pleasure looked discontented, plucked their hats over their eyes, and were much perplexed, foreseeing that their being here must inevitably vanish. Those that had lain under a cloud for several years behind appear with cheerful looks; while others, that had then flourished, drooped away or withdrew themselves privately, they knowing very well that they had eaten other men's bread, and that, if they should stay, should undergo a visitation and censure by those men that they had themselves formerly visited. The common people hugged themselves up with the thoughts of a king and of renewing their good old cause, enjoyed their sports, especially May-games, more this year than hath been since, chiefly in opposition to Presbyterians and fanatics, who had shown great anger before towards them. Further also they left nothing undone whereby they might express their joy, and the more because they had been severely kept under by the Presbyterian discipline; and glad many were that they had this opportunity of shaking it off The Common Prayer Book and surplice were restored in every church and chapel; and the service that had been lately practised, viz. a psalm or two, two chapters, and a prayer of the priest's own making, with a little more, laid aside. All tokens of monarchy that were lately defaced or obscured in the university were also restored and new furbished over; and whatsoever was as yet fit to be introduced many did not spare to effect, and some to outrun and overdo the law before the King or Parliament had put it in force.'

Notwithstanding the cordial approbation with which he regarded the general conduct of the restorers, even so thorough-going a partisan as Antony Wood puts it beyond question that the Visitors, in their zeal for the Cavaliers and their detestation of Puritanism, were guilty in exceptional instances of gross injustice and flagrant disregard of law. 'All fellows,' says Antony, admitting in his contradictory statements probably more than he intended against the instruments of Royalist vengeance, ' and scholars of each house that were living unmarried, they restored, ejecting these divers, *especially such that were factious or not fit to make collegiates, notwithstanding they had been statutably elected*; and all, whether fellows scholars, servants, &c. that they restored, did not amount to the sixth part of those ejected 1648, and after: they being either dead, or married, or had changed their religion. But before I proceed to speak of that tithe, which is left behind, I shall observe this, that whereas great cruelty was acted in the Presbyterian Visitation twelve years before, now nothing but moderation, and a requital in a manner of good for evil in this. And indeed few or none could find reason to complain of what was done by these Visitors; for the persons that had been ejected were to be restored, *and room was to be made for them; to which end some, though statutably elected since* 1648, were ejected; yet provision was made for divers of them, if they would accept it, as chaplains' places in some colleges, and clerks in others.'

After this rigmarole, Antony goes on to show how the visitors ' requited in a manner good for evil' at Lincoln College, where they ejected five statutably elected fellows, though no Cavalier ventured to assert that he had been ejected by the Parliamentarian Commissioners from any one of the fellowships thus rendered vacant by an iniquitous abuse of power.

The case of the five Lincoln fellows deserves special commemoration, for the circumstances of their expulsion illustrate the animus with which the Visitors discharged their judicial functions, and exhibit, in a remarkable manner, the ferocious intolerance of the restorers.

At Lincoln College there was not a single claimant for the place held by any one of the fellows. Death or marriage had removed from the original number of the Royalist scholars ejected in 1648 every man who, had the Restoration occurred ten years earlier, would have been in a position to demand that he should be restored to the Lincoln fellowship, from which he had been ousted by the saints. Five fellows, however, were expelled from the college, though nothing worse could be proved against them than that they were disliked by the rector, and had incurred the hatred of two fellows who were his obsequious creatures.

Paul Hood, D.D., the Rector, who conspired with two scheming sycophants to deprive five fellow-collegians of their academic preferment, was a remarkable specimen of the class of politico-religious turncoats, for whom the satire of a previous century had invented the nickname of 'Vicars of Bray Elected to his office under James the First, he had been an orthodox Churchman during Laud's supremacy, had joined heartily with the Puritans on the downfall of the first Charles, and towards the dose of the Interregnum had played his cards so adroitly that he was made one of the Visitors appointed to reform Oxford in 1660. The man who thus cleverly ' closed with the times' was a doctor in dissimulation as well as divinity, and he was not more odious for deceitfulness than for rancorous vindictiveness. No less despotic in his college than servile to authority outside its walls, he had quarrelled on sundry trivial matters with the fellows whose expulsion he persuaded his colleagues in the commission of Visitors to regard as requisite for the well-being of the house, of which he was the governor. The delinquents were factious persons, whose disposition was altogether favourable to rebellion and anarchy. In support of his assertions to their discredit, the accuser, who was also one of the judges of the gentlemen whom he vilified, called in evidence two kindred informers and renegades, fellows of Dr. Hook's house, who, 'though they had been notorious complyers,' says Wood, 'yet now, forsooth, in hopes of preferment and honours, had faced about, and become wonderful zealots in the prelatical cause.'

The conspiracy succeeded beyond the hopes of the conspirators; and four of the expelled collegians, submitting meekly to their fate, retired from their college without exasperating their triumphant enemies by futile resistance. But the fifth victim, George Hitchcocke, held his ground with a firmness that reminded the university of the way in which the Cavalier scholars had defied the Puritan visitors twelve years earlier. The result was the liveliest and smartest little row that the scholars had witnessed for many a day. Ordered to quit the college, the resolute Mr. Hitchcocke derided the command, and continued to draw his commons from kitchen and buttery, as though nothing had happened to weaken his title to food and entertainment at the expense of the house. To a yeoman-bedell who entered Lincoln College to arrest him, Mr. Hitchcocke responded by drawing a rapier and threatening to take the life of any one who should venture to lay hands upon him. Whereupon the yeoman-bedell turned pale, descended the staircase by which the desperado's chamber was approached, and told Dr. Hood that the arrest of so violent a scholar should be entrusted to the military. Taking the same view of the crisis, Dr. Hood hired eight soldiers and their captain, who agreed for the moderate sum of twenty shillings to go into action against the redoubtable Hitchcocke, blow open with gunpowder the door of his barricaded rooms, and drive him from the college with the smallest possible sacrifice of life. The compact between learning and arms was fulfilled. Having forced their way into the scholar's chamber, the military called upon him to surrender at discretion. Instead of complying, Mr. Hitchcocke threw himself upon the captain of the storming party, whilst his friends —Mr. Hamlet Puliston, of Jesus College, and Mr. Christopher Pyke, gentleman commoner of Lincoln College—showed a commendable readiness to shed quite as much blood as the occasion would justify. But the fight ended almost before it had begun. Mr. Hitchcocke was 'pinked' in the arm, and lost a finger in the fray; a sword-blow gave an effective gash to Mr. Pyke's skull. Mr. Puliston was disabled and disarmed before he had done or suffered any serious mischief; and in less than a quarter of an hour from the commencement of the affair, Mr. Hitchcocke was lodged in the prison, whence after several weeks of confinement he retreated to an inn of court, where he applied himself to the study of the law, which had been so impotent to secure him from flagrant outrage and great wrong.

After their recapture of Oxford the Cavaliers were loudly jubilant in the colleges and schools; but I am not in a position to record that they raised the moral tone or intellectual reputation of the university, which for many a day was less regarded as a place of strenuous study than as a centre of political feeling. That the restored scholars and the gownsmen, who cooperated with them in determining the tone of the colleges, comprised many men of sincere piety and high attainments is certain;

but upon the whole they evinced more concern for liquor than learning, and were of opinion that scholarship was a less important requisite than political orthodoxy in candidates for places on collegiate foundations. Their darling preacher and wit, Dr. South, won their applause with sermons that sparkled with jocular allusions to affairs of state, and insisted that no circumstances could justify subjects in resisting the tyranny of their divinely appointed rulers: and whilst the epigrammatic divine expressed his detestation of the Protector, whom he had formerly extolled in a scholastic exercise, and declared his abhorrence of the cruel and bloodthirsty people concerned in the rebellion against Charles the Martyr, he seized frequent occasions to throw ridicule on the Royal Society, which, having come into existence during 'the late troubles and having acquired vigour in Cromwel-lian Oxford, was naturally regarded with suspicion and disdain by the more enthusiastic opponents of innovation. Like the ' Sons of the Ministers which originated in the days of the Interregnum and was refashioned by the Royalists of the Restoration, so as to bring it into accord with prelatical sentiment, the Royal Society was reorganized and reconstituted under Charles the Second; but though Oxford of the nineteenth century points to it proudly as one of her contributions to the intellectual life of modern England, the association for the furtherance of natural science was held in no cordial esteem by the Restorers.

Nor can I imagine that the moral health of the university derived advantage from the favour accorded to it by the merry monarch, whose sojournings in the seat of learning occasioned scandal to serious and devout students, and taught ingenuous youth that the supreme governor of the Church might openly violate the first rules of morality, without losing the good opinion of society or provoking censure from his prelates. Catharine of Braganza's residence in Merton College, with the ladies of her suite, was very agreeable to the principals and tutors, who, looking backward over years of trouble and banishment, could recall the time when Henrietta Maria had maintained similar state in the same palace; but besides contributing to the life of the colleges and the gaiety of the town, the presence of the Queen's court occasioned some rather unwholesome though pungent gossip in halls and common rooms, when Lady Castlemaine, in all the splendour of triumphant beauty and all the effrontery of shameless wickedness, appeared in Oxford, whither she followed the King, so soon as she could safely rise from the bed on which she had given birth to the first Duke of Grafton.

How Oxford and Oxonian ways struck the few intelligent foreigners who visited the university at this brilliant if not altogether honourable period of its history, may be inferred from the tone of Monsieur Samuel Sorbiere's reflections on academic men and manners in his ' Voyage to England: Containing Many Things Relating to the State of Learning, Religion, and other Curiosities of that Kingdom;' a narrative of travel which gained for its author a sentence of exile from his native country, and elicited a reply from Thomas Pratt, Bishop of Rochester. The French physician visited England in 1664; and in his account of the islanders,—a treatise almost as completely forgotten as the contro-versy which it provoked,—the tourist wrote, 'The doctor' (*i.e.*, Wallis, the Savilian Professor of logical notoriety) 'has less in him of the gallant man than Mr. Hobbs; and if you should see him with his university cap on his head, as if he had a portefeuille on, covered with black cloth, and sewed to his Calot, you would be as much inclined to laugh at his diverting society as you would be ready to ascertan the excellency and civility of my friend with esteem and affection. What I have said concerning Dr. Wallis is not intended in the least to derogate from the praises due to one of the greatest mathematicians in the world; and who being no more than forty years of age may advance his studies much farther, and become polite, if purified by the air of the court at London. For I must tell you, sir, that that of the university stands in need of it ; and that those who are purified other ways, have naturally strong breaths, that are noxious in conversation. This I plainly discerned by having an opportunity to compare this subtle and learned professor with Mr. Lockey, the Oxford Librarian, who had learnt at court and in France to put on an obliging air and courteous behaviour. He had the goodness not only to conduct me to the library, but all the colledges, and to introduce me to all the professors I visited. I lodged in Christ Church, which is the largest and richest of them all, its income being 70,000 livres a-year. Cardinal Wolsey built it in the reign of Henry the VIII., of whom he was such a favourite that that prince built Hampton Court for him, which is now a royal palace, twelve miles from London. There are seventeen or eighteen colledges at Oxford, which are almost all of the same dimensions, they are built of free-stone. The meanest of them is not inferior to the Sorbonne, for there are some of them that do excel it. The lower court of Christ Church Colledge is little less than that which is contained within the barriers of the Place Royale. There is a physick-garden over against St. Catharine's, to-wards the gate that leads to London, which is small, ill-kept, and. more like an orchard than a garden. I shall not take upon me to describe all the colledges to you. There is one, at whose gate I saw a great brazen-nose, like Punchinello's vizard I was told they also call it Brazen-Nose Colledge, and that John Dunscotus taught here, in remembrance of which they set up the sign of his nose at, the gate. The last colledge I visited was St. John's, which is the most regular building of any of them, though not the richest. It has two square courts, as large as the square we now have in the Louvre, and two large buildings, three story high, with four wings of the same height: I saw a fine library in one of them, and a large wainscotted gallery, wherein I found no other ornament than the picture of King Charles I., which they took out of a cover, and showed here for a rarity, because the hair of his head was made up of Scripture lines, wrought wonderfully small, and more particularly of the Psalms of David in Latin. This prince, and the queen mother's statues in brass, stand in the second court upon the two gates: and the two late Archbishops of Canterbury, who were benefactors to this colledge, are buried in the chapel: there are two large gardens belonging to this colledge, one of which is terrassed, and the other faces a plain to the northward. The famous library of Oxford, where their public lectures are read, requires we should dwell a long while on the subject: it is made in the form of an H, has two stories of books: the lowermost has six rows of folios, and three of quartos; in the other, to which you get up by wooden stairs, very artfully contrived for to give light in the middle, and at the four corners, there are nine rows more, whereof three of folios, and the rest of different volumes : those of Selden are on one side, together with the manuscripts given to the library by the late Arch-bishop Laud, being two thousand four hundred in number. We took a walk in the galleries over the library, and saw a great number of medals there, and there are the pictures of some learned men round the galleries, where they showed us the sword which the Pope sent Henry VIII. as defender of the Faith. Here is a place of anatomy not worth seeing: the schools were all of them shut up, and there are scarce any lectures read there, because the private ones draw all the scholars thither. Oxford city would be nothing without the colledges: for there are scarce any more inhabitants in it than are enough to serve three or four thousand students: and to cultivate a very delightful plain, where the city stands upon a small river, abounding with fish, which falls near it into the Thames. We were two days in going by the stage to Oxford, through a fine country, where we were delighted with the sight of Uxbridge, Beconfields, High Wickham, which they call towns, though they are in strictness nothing more than large unwalled boroughs. They frightened us with the danger of highwaymen on the road, which I thought they did out of vanity, and to the end that Paris might have nothing to upbraid London with : but I am satisfied that some of them appeared in reality now and then. It is certain there are good regulations made in this country; and when any robbery is committed, the country people presently take the alarm, and pursue so hard, that the highwaymen very seldom can make their escape

The reader of those passages of this work which relate to the number of the Oxonian scholars in the seventeenth century, does not need to be told how greatly the tourist was at fault in computing the students of Charles the Second's Oxford at between three and four thousand. Monsieur Sorbiere's exaggeration of the academic population would, however, have appeared sufficiently truthful to the majority of the educated Englishmen whom he encountered in his travels, and was perhaps due to the statements of Oxford dons who, when showing him Alma Mater's objects of interest, felt themselves bound to magnify her importance.

CHAPTER X

THE SHELDONIAN THEATRE.

IN their long conflict throughout the period of ecclesiastical reformation and the following century, the Puritans and Anglican High-Churchmen were guilty of striking inconsistencies of demeanour and doctrine with respect to several of the matters about which they contended most fiercely. Whilst the more zealous Puritans reprobated the superstitious observance of days, and reflected bitterly on the respect which their opponents exhibited for times set apart for the commemoration of saints, they were remarkable for the severity with which they kept the weekly holiday, as a sacred period on which no man could without sin follow worldly business. On the other hand, whilst he celebrated with religious mourning and festivity days which the Precisians regarded with indifference, the High-Churchman of Elizabethan or Laudian England never ceased to ridicule the mental confusion and fanatical error which caused the Puritans to observe the first day in the week with doleful austerity, and to maintain that Christians were bound to keep the Sunday in accordance with the rules laid down for the celebration of the Jewish Sabbath.

It was the same with respect to sacred buildings, and the reverence in which they should be held by devout persons. Though the movement, which resulted eventually in the discontinuance of the social use of the churches, had originated with the Lollards, and was reluctantly adopted by the Elizabethan ecclesiastics, the High-Churchmen of the earlier decades of the seventeenth century claimed credit for their devout care of holy places, and reproached the Puritans for their readiness to profane the temples of the living God, and for their impiety in maintaining that public houses of worship differed chiefly from ordinary houses in having steeples instead of chimneys. Even while he favoured Sunday-sports, though held in the immediate precincts of churches, and allowed the inhabitants of rural parishes to hold their church-ales under the roofs of their churches, when they could not conveniently provide themselves with church-houses, Laud was indefatigable in restoring and decorating the national fanes, and in instructing the people to exhibit worshipful reverence for the buildings dedicated to religious uses. With the fervour of a fourteenth century Lollard, or an Elizabethan reformer, he raised his voice against divers social uses which tended to the profanation of churches. He put rails round the communion tables, encouraged the general adoption of pews, enjoined church-wardens to be prompt in correcting the customary disorderliness of congregations, and, amongst other edicts for main-taining the sanctity of churches, forbade that they should be used as courts of justice. Whilst the primate thus bestirred himself to renovate and adorn the temples, and to exalt the popular estimation of their sacredness, the opposition which he encountered from the Puritans was construed by his adherents as evidence of the Puritanical tendency to desecrate all holy things.

It is needless to remark that no such inference could be justly drawn from the action and teaching of the moderate Puritans, who, in due course, put Laud's party to the rout, or even from the iconoclastic outrages of the zealots who, during the rage of the civil war, exhibited their righteous enthusiasm by barbarously destroying a considerable number of the painted windows and other works of art with which the ecclesiastical restorers had adorned the churches in times subsequent to the reformation. Though the wilder sectarians of the period might talk derisively of steeple-houses, no lack of reverence and devout affection for places of worship was observable in the congregations who thronged the churches during the Commonwealth, and cordially preferred the services of the Directory to those of the Common Prayer. The generality of the discreet, demure, sober Precisians, who delighted in long prayers and longer sermons, protracted readings of scripture and an abundance of congregational psalmody, had nothing or very little in common with the mobs of image-breakers, whose excesses were not more due to spiritual phrensy than to constitutional destructiveness. On many points they were perverse, narrow, and stubborn, but their peculiar orderliness disposed them to regard with strong disfavour whatever tended to want of religious decorum. They removed from places of worship the crosses, pictures, and ritualistic para-phernalia which, in their opinion, tended to promote superstition and mislead the simple. Their delight in outward simplicity impelled them to obliterate mural paintings and cover the variegated surface of superb marble pillars with coats of white-wash. They allowed cathedrals to drop into decay, and even deliberated whether it would not be well to destroy them; but far from arising from any malignant disposition to desecrate holy things, their neglect of the dilapidated cathedrals, and their inclination to pull them down, sprung from a sincere belief that the edifices were no longer capable of rendering religious service to mankind, were, on the contrary, calculated to do society spiritual mischief, and had therefore altogether lost whatever sacredness pertained to them in former time.

But, on their return to power with Charles the Second, the royalist Episcopalians very generally concurred in representing that the Puritans were the enemies of true religion, and had always manifested a diabolical pleasure in desecrating temples and defaming priests. The sectarians had abhorred Laud chiefly because he courageously denounced their profanity, and laboured to cleanse the churches of mundane defilements. Though many of the angry utterers of this ridiculous historic fiction must have known that, in discouraging or prohibiting the social use of the churches, the primate had merely endeavoured to use for his ends the sentiment and the movement which had originated with his adversaries, they employed all the artifices of misrepresentation to make it accepted as veritable history. Remembering that in the civil war each party had in turn used sacred buildings for military purposes, they had the effrontery to assert that the Puritan com-manders, who quartered their soldiers in cathedrals and mounted their guns on church-towers, were in so doing guilty of impious enormities which no general of the martyred king's army had perpetrated. Pointing to the dilapidations of cathedrals, and diverting attention from the cleanliness and soundness of the parochial churches, the accusers said that the disroofed and dismantled walls of the venerable fanes demonstrated the atrocious nature of the reprobates who had murdered their sovereign and despoiled the church in the name of religion. Pointing to relics of the ancient social use of churches — customs that, originating in mediaeval times, had survived successive ecclesiastical changes and contrived to hold their ground during the Commonwealth— the denouncers of presbytery and independency declared that these practices, which the Puritans had merely forborne to abolish, had sprung up during the confusion of the late troubles, and at the order of canting Roundheads. One has heard somewhat too much of the hypocrisy of the Puritans, but scarcely enough of the sanctimonious cant of their opponents. In the seventeenth century the hypocrites who wore sad clothes and spoke through the nose were not more unscrupulous than the hypocrites whose talk implied that no layman could be sincerely religious unless he wore long hair and indulged in modish blasphemy.

Whilst this cant was the newest feshion, the Oxonian Royalists, who had been largely instrumental in bringing it into vogue, discovered that it would be a desecration to continue to use St. Mary's Church for such scholastic exercises and secular pomps as had been performed in it from the earliest existence of the edifice. It was in accordance with their characteristic profanity for the puritanical hypocrites to have made no more account of the university church than if it had been an unconsecrated lecture-hall; but it was not for the restorers of Episcopacy and true religion to imitate the iniquitous proceedings of the rebellious Nonconformists. To what a degree this humbug prevailed amongst the Oxonians of the Restoration, may be inferred from the fact that Antony Wood consented to give it countenance in the same sentence of his *Annals*, in which, to save his antiquarian knowledge from ridicule, he was also careful to remark that the profane action, attributed to the saints, had been a feature of academic life ' beyond all memory.' The annalist says—* Upon the restoration of King Charles II., and soon after of divers members of the university that had been ejected in 1648, thoughts were entertained by them and others of erecting some public fabric, wherein the Act exercises that were and had been performed beyond all memory in St. Mary's Church, might, with better convenience and according to the dignity of the university, be celebrated; and the house of God, which had been too much profaned by the sacrilege of those times during the rebellion, might hereafter be wholly employed to sacred uses. Animated thereunto by the piety of the design, and the exhortation of divers eminent persons, especially those bishops that had been formerly members of the university, were bought of the citizens divers houses standing on the place where formerly the trench and ditch ran under their wall, to the end that room might be made for the said fabric: which being done about the latter end of the year 1663, they were pulled down, together with the university's embattled wall that parted them from the area lying before the convocation-house door, and on the north side of the Divinity School

The project was very popular with the gownsmen. Bishops were of opinion that the undertaking would redound to the honour of Oxford, and promote piety throughout the whole kingdom. There was no doubt in the minds of prelates and principals, tutors and students, that so soon as the building was begun funds would flow in for its completion from every palace and parsonage that sheltered scholars interested in Alma Mater's glory. The Archbishop had consented to be chief patron of the architectural movement, and what better patron for so sincere and altogether honest a scheme, for the revival of religion and the discomfiture of the Puritans, could there be than the Cavalier primate, of whom Bishop Burnet wrote—'He seemed not to have a deep sense of religion, if any at all; and spoke of it most commonly as an engine of government, and a matter of policy V Every one allowed that the spiritually disposed Sheldon was the natural director of the affair; and taking the same view of the matter, the archbishop sent the university the very handsome donation of one thousand pounds, and recommended that Dr. Christopher Wren should be requested to prepare a design for the edifice, and put it in effect. Christopher "Wren was quite willing to accept the commission; and every one approved the proposals of the future architect of St. Paul's cathedral The first stones of the foundation of the theatre were laid in 1664 with suitable pomp, speeches, and music, by trowel-handling prelates, who performed their masonic tasks to the cordial approval of a numerous and scholarly multitude of spectators. With one exception, the enterprise was a success in all its particulars; but that one exception affected Gilbert Sheldon's pocket and feme in a very singular manner.

Of all the divines and notabilities who applauded the movement, no one thought right to follow the primate's example by contributing liberally to the fund for building. The subscription was a signal failure. In justice to the men, who were so much more lavish of fair words than of hard money, it must be remembered that, though holding high ecclesiastical preferments or considerable estates, they were by no means flush of cash. The bishops and deans had succeeded to offices, the emoluments of which were greatly curtailed by the effects of the civil troubles. They had found it necessary to spend large sums on the repair of their residences, to contribute money towards the restoration of their cathedrals, and to meet a variety of unanticipated demands. The rebellion had so grievously impoverished the Royalist families, that nearly every Cavalier, fortunate enough to procure a lucrative office or to possess a few farms, was burdened with debts contracted during the Interregnum, or was under obligations to assist necessitous relatives, who, like himself, had been pecuniary sufferers from the rebellion. Moreover, the social fashions of the period were eminently calculated to exhaust the finances of persons who were required to make some figure before the world. The ugly fact, however, remained: Christopher Wren had been employed to build the grand theatre; and, besides Archbishop Sheldon and a few subscribers of trivial sums, no one cared to give the architect so much as a single broad-piece. After all the big talk to the dis-honour of the Puritans and the glorification of Episcopacy, the monetary disappointment was likely to raise a laugh against the university.

What was to be done? It was of importance that the theatre should be built, but it was impossible to build it without funds. Whence should the funds come ? Society answered, from the primate who had committed his reputation to the success of the project. Circumstances induced the archbishop to take the same view of the difficulty. He was fairly ' let in' for the expense; and, seeing that he was not likely to derive much material aid from subscribers, he determined to bear the whole cost of the work, and, making a virtue of what was almost a necessity, gain credit for princely munificence. ' The archbishop,' says Wood, ' having been thus noble, it was hoped that others would have succeeded unto the example; but these expectations being frustrate, the archbishop took the whole matter on himself, and paid all, to a farthing, both for the out and inside thereof, as also for the furniture and utensils belonging to it' I am not aware of the existence of any evidence that the primate resented for any long period the misgodliness of the Oxonians who left him to pay for the theatre, toward the expense of which he had been assured that they would contribute promptly; but Evelyn informs us that instead of watching with interest the growth or surveying with pride the completeness of the building, on which he spent 25,000*l*., Dr. Sheldon (who, by the way, became chancellor of the university, on Lord Clarendon's fall, whilst the theatre was in course of construction) determined never to look on the result of his not altogether spontaneous miinificence. 'It was never seen by the benefactor,' says the diarist, ' my lord-archbishop having told me that he never did or ever would see it.'

The fabric of the theatre was well-nigh completed in June, 1668, the month in which Samuel Pepys, together with his wife, made the trip to Oxford, concerning which he entered in his diary, ' 9th (Tuesday). We came to Oxford, a very sweet place; paid our guide *ll*.2*s*.6*d*.; barber, 2*s*.6*d*; book, *Stonehenge*, 4s.; boy that showed me the colleges before dinner, Is. To dinner, and then out with my wife and people, and landlord; and to him that showed us the schools and library, 10s.; to him that showed us All Souls' College and Chichly's picture, 5s. Go to see Christ Church with my wife, I seeing several others very fine alone, before dinner, and did give the boy that went with me Is. Strawberries, Is. 2*d*.; dinner and servants, 1*l* 0s. 6*d*. After coming home from the schools, I out with the landlord to Brasenose College; to the butteries, and in the hand of the child of Hales, . . . long. Butler, 2s. Thence with coach and people to see the physic-garden, 1s. So to Friar Bacon's study: I up and saw it, and gave the man 1s. Bottle of sack for landlord, 1s. Oxford mighty fine place, and well seated, and cheap entertainment. At night came to Abingdon, where had been a fair of custard, and met many people and scholars going home; and there did get some pretty good musick, and sang and danced till supper, 5s.' Unless Pepys's superabundance of vanity impelled him to ' tip' the lacqueys and guides more liberally than custom required him to do, the foregoing entries must be held to indicate that sight-seers were mercilessly fleeced in Charles the Second's Oxford. When the value of money in the seventeenth century is considered, some of the diarist's payments in the university appear exorbitant; and yet he extols the cheapness of his entertainment.

Some seven or eight months later the 'Diary' enables us to accompany Pepys to Serjeant Painter Streeter's studio, where that 'famous history-painter' is at work on the paintings which he has been com-missioned to paint ' for the new theatre at Oxford,' concerning which artistic performances the diarist observes, ' and, indeed, they look as if they would be very fine, and the rest think better than those of Rubens in the Banqueting House at White Hall, but I do not so fully think so. But they will certainly be very noble; and I am mightily pleased to have the fortune to see this man and his work, which is very famous; and he a very civil little man, and lame, but lives very handsomely

In the July of 1669, the academic authorities took formal possession of the completed and richly-fitted theatre, when Sheldon's munificence and Alma Mater's gratitude were celebrated with an entertainment of scholastic exercises, recitations, and music, in the presence of the dense assemblage of academicians and sight-seers from the country, who found seats or standing-room in the edifice. John Evelyn, the diarist, was one of the distinguished persons who received honorary degrees on the occasion of this academic festival, of which he has given us the following graphic account:—

' 9th. In the morning was celebrated the' Encaenia of the New Theatre, so magnificently built by the munificence of Dr. Gilbert Sheldon, Archbishop of Canterbury, in which was spent 25,000*l*., as Sir Christopher Wren, the architect (as I remember), told me; and yet it was never seen by the benefactor, my Lord Archbishop having told me that he never did or ever would see it. It is, in truth, a fabric comparable to any of this kind of former ages, and doubtless exceeding any of the present, as this University does for colleges, libraries, schools, students, and order, all the universities in the world. To the theatre is added the famous Sheldonian Printing House. This being at the Act, and at the first time of opening the theatre (Acts being formerly kept in St. Mary's Church, which might be thought indecent, that being a place set apart for the immediate worship of God, and was the inducement for building this noble pile), it was now resolved, to keep the present Act in it, and celebrate its dedication with the greatest splendour and formality that might be,; and, therefore, drew a world of strangers, and other company, to the University, from all parts of the nation.

'The Vice-Chancelior, heads of houses, and doc-tors, being seated in magisterial seats, the Vice-Chancellor's chair and desk, proctors, &c, covered with brocatelle (a kind of brocade) and cloth of gold, the University Registrar read the founder's grant and gift of it to the university for their scholastic exercises upon these solemn occasions. Then followed Dr. South, the university's orator, in an eloquent speech, which was very long and not without some malicious and indecent, reflections on the Royal Society, as underminers. of the university; which was very foolish and untrue, as well as unreasonable. But, to let that pass from an ill-natured man, the rest was in praise of the archbishop and the ingenious architect. This ended, after loud music from the corridor above, where an organ was placed, there followed divers panegyric speeches, both in prose and verse, interchangeably pronounced by the young students placed in the rostrums, in pindarics, eclogues, heroics, &c, mingled with excellent music, vocal and instrumental, to entertain the ladies and the rest of the company. A speech was then made in praise of academical learning. This lasted from eleven in the morning till seven at night, which was concluded with ringing of bells and universal joy and feasting.

'10th July. The next day began the more solemn lectures in all the faculties, which were performed in the several schools, where all the Inceptor-Doctors did their exercises, the professors having first ended their reading. The assembly now returned to the theatre, where the Terræ Filius (the university buffoon) entertained the auditory with a tedious, abusive, sarcastical rhapsody, most unbecoming the gravity of the university, and that so grossly, that, unless it be suppressed, it will be of ill consequence, as I afterwards plainly expressed my sense of it to the Vice-Chancellor and several heads of houses, who were perfectly ashamed of it, and resolved to take care of it in future. The old facetious way of rallying upon the questions was left off, falling wholly upon persons, so that it was rather licentious lying railing than genuine and noble wit. In my life I was never witness of so shameful entertainment.

'After this ribaldry, the proctors made their speeches, then began the music art, vocal and in-strumental, above in the balustrade corridor opposite to the Vice-Chancellor's chair. Then Dr. Wallis, the Mathematical Professor, made his oration, and created one doctor of music according to the usual ceremonies of gown (which was of white damask), cap, ring, kiss, &c. Next followed the disputations of the In-ceptor-Doctors in Medicine, the speech of their professor, Dr. Hyde, and so in course their respective creations. Then disputed the In-ceptors of Law, the speech of their professor, and creation. Lastly, Inceptors of Theology: Dr. Comp-ton (brother to the Earl of Northampton), being junior, began with great modesty and applause; so the rest After which, Dr. Tillotson, Dr. Sprat, &c., and then Dr. Allestree's speech, the King's Professor, and their respective creations. Last of all, the Vice-chancellor, shutting up the whole in a panegyrical oration, celebrating their benefactor and the rest, apposite to the occasion.

' Thus was the theatre dedicated by the scholastic exercises in all the faculties with great solemnity; and the night, as the former, entertaining the new doctors' friends in feasting and music. I was invited by Dr. Barlow, the worthy and learned Professor of Queen's College.

' 11th July. The Act Sermon was this forenoon preached by Dr. Hall, in St. Mary's, in an honest practical discourse against atheism. In the afternoon the church was so crowded that, not coming early, I could not approach to hear.

12th July, Monday. Was held the Divinity Act in the theatre again, when proceeded seventeen doctors, in all the faculties some.

' 13th. I dined at the Vice-Chancellor's, and spent the afternoon in seeing the rarities of the public libraries, and visiting the noble marbles and inscriptions, now inserted in the walls that compass the area of the theatre, which were 150 of most ancient and worthy treasures of that kind in the learned world. Now, observing that people approach them too near, some idle persons began to scratch and injure them, I advised that a hedge of holly should be planted at the foot of the wall, to be kept breast-high only, to protect them, which the Vice-Chancellor promised to do the next season.

'14th. Dr. Fell, Dean of Christ Church, and Vice-Chancellor, with Dr. Allestree, Professor, with beadles and maces before them, came to visit me at my lodging. I went to visit Lord Howard's sons at Magdalen College.

' 15th. Having two days before had notice that the university intended me the honour of doctorship, I was this morning attended by the beadles belonging to the Law, who conducted me to the theatre, where I found the Duke of Ormond (now Chancellor of the University), with the Earl of Chesterfield and Mr. Spencer (brother to the late Earl of Sunderland). Thence we marched to the Convocation-house, a convocation having been called on purpose; here, being all of us robed in the porch, in scarlet, with caps and hoods, we were led in by the Professor of Laws, and presented respectively by name, with a short eulogy, to the Vice-Chancellor, who sat in the chair, with all the doctors and heads of houses and masters about the room, which was exceeding full. Then began the public orator his speech, directed chiefly to the Duke of Ormond, the Chancellor, but in which I had my compliment in course. This ended, we were called up, and created doctors according to the form, and seated by. the Vice-Chancellor amongst the doctors on his right hand; then the Vice-Chancellor made a short speech, and so, saluting our brother doctors, the pageantry concluded, and the convocation was dissolved. So formal a creation of honorary doctors had seldom been seen, that a convocation should be called on purpose, and speeches made by the orator; but they could not do less, their Chancellor being to receive, or rather do them this honour. I should have been made doctor with the rest at the public act, but their expectation of their chancellor made them defer it. I was then led with my brother doctors to an extraordinary entertainment at Doctor Mewes', head of St. John's College ; and, after abundance of feasting and compliments, having visited the Vice-Chancellor and other doctors, and given them thanks for the honour done me, I went towards home the 16th, and got as far as Windsor, and so to my house the next day.

In the time intervening between the opening of the Sheldonian theatre and the prevalence of the modern novel, young men of literary aspirations, on coming to London fresh from college, were wont to try their 'prentice hands at writing, and exhibit their, knowledge of life, by illustrating the humours of the universities in dramatic works, just as, in these more recent days of the popularity of prose fiction, they are accustomed to work up their knowledge of human nature and manners at Oxford or Cambridge into volumes of romantic narrative. And in the plays thus produced some five or six generations since, by literary aspirants of university education, the reader, given to perusing forgotten writings, comes every now and then on allusions to the Sheldonian theatre, and even on scenes laid in the building. For instance, in 'An Act at Oxford, a Comedy, by the author of the " Yeoman o' Kent,' one of the principal scenes is the interior of the Sheldonian Theatre, during the performance of the annual exercises, with a display, sufficient for dramatic illusion, of doctors, undergraduates, and lionesses. This comedy, entitled also ' Hampstead Heath,' was put upon the boards at Drury Lane; and notwithstanding its lack of humour and smartness, the piece was so popular that an edition of the work having been published in 1704, there was a demand for a second edition which appeared in 1706.

CHAPTER XI

GARDENS AND WALKS.

NOOKS and corners of garden may still be found in Oxford, where gownsmen munched pears and plucked flowers generations, and even centuries, before Sir Robert Chambers—whilom Vinerian Professor of Law and Principal of New Inn Hall— provoked an expostulation from Dr. Johnson by throwing snails over the boundary-wall of his ornamental enclosure into the adjoining flower-garden of an obnoxious neighbour. 'Sir,' exclaimed the dictionary-maker, abruptly and hotly, 'your conduct is unmannerly and unneighbourly. Justifying himself, as he pitched another handful of the molluscs over the wall, the Principal of New Inn replied, ' Sir, my neighbour is a dissenter ' Oh; returned the doctor, his sense of humour and his political intolerance getting the better of his regard for neighbourliness, ' if so, Chambers, toss away, as hard as you can

But though Oxonian principals and dons still expend horticultural care on cosy plots of ground, which yielded fruit and flowers to scholars in the days of the Tudors and earlier Stuarts, the spacious and pleasant gardens, that contribute so largely to the external attractiveness of the university, are of comparatively recent construction. The work of New Oxford, they bear the evidence of their origin in the curving lines of their umbrageous paths, emerald lawns, and bright parterres, and in the disposition of their timber, planted and cherished in accordance with the principles of the school of landscape-gardeners who flourished in the eighteenth century, and with the aid of Horace Walpole's critical patronage drove the geometrical garden, with its hard lines, grotesque devices, and unnatural angles, less quickly than completely out of fashion.

How little Oxford of the seventeenth century was indebted to horticulture for the European fame of her outward loveliness, the reader may ascertain by referring to David Loggan's ' Oxonia Illustrata,'¹ a collection of engravings that are the appropriate illustrative accompaniment to Antony Wood's annals of the academic life of his own time.

Whilst turning over the leaves of the 'Oxonia Illustrata,' the Oxonian of the nineteenth century, who remembers the English version of the Rustica Descriptio is tempted to repeat John Allibond's lines,

 The glory wert thou of our land,
 Oh, Oxford ! and honoured thy name !
 How is it (I can't understand)
 Though the same that thou art not the same.

As he passes through the streets of the university, he recognizes college after college, but each house presents some peculiarity which rouses his curiosity and perplexes his judgment. Now and then the discrepancies between the pictorial representations and his own experience arise from the presence of unfamiliar features, but more frequently from the absence of well-known objects, in the portraitures of buildings whose general characteristics are faithfully rendered by the artist's cunning. This college wants a third of its frontage and two-thirds of its residential buildings; another has its distinguished gateway, but overhead there is neither belfry nor tower; a third, like an old friend with a new face, is scarcely recognizable from its streetward aspect, whilst its interior structure has not altered in appearance by so much as a single stone.

Nor is the visitor of Loggan's Oxford less struck by the life of the thoroughfares, than by what is new and unanticipated in the look of the colleges. Far from the days of railways, and remote also from the era of turn-pike roads, and stagecoaches pledged to travel at the rate of twelve miles an hour², he hears no continual or gen-

---

1 Oxonia lllnstrata. Sire omnium celeberrim® istius Univer-sitatis Collegiarum, Aularum, Bibliothecae Bodleianae, Scholarum Pnblicarum, Theatri Sheldoniani, nec non Urbis toting Scenographia. Delineavit et sculpsit Day. Loggan, Univ. Oxon. Chal-cographus, 1675.

2 The Flying Coach' of Charles the Second's Oxford did not travel twelve miles an hour, but its

eral sound of wheels in the High but in place thereof a constant clattering of packhorses walking or ambling on the rough pavement. Smart hansoms, ramshackle flies, clattering carts, luxurious phaetons are nowhere visible. Here at the gate of some scholastic house, let us say All Souls, where it has deposited some six or eight head of quality, who are paying their respects to the Warden's lady, is standing a ponderous and flagrantly embellished ark on wheels, which has been drawn to its present position by four big, long-legged, long-tailed, broad-chested Flemish mares; and yonder comes the Vice-Chancellor's coach, drawn by six horses, that know by experience that the six of them are not at all too many to convey their owner and his equally preposterous and majestic vehicle, together with its proper complement of liveried servants, to a dinner-party at any of the great county houses lying within six or eight miles of St Mary's Church. But though these lordly equipages, with their superabundance of heraldic pictures and other orna-ments, help to give an air of patrician splendour to the High Street, and inform the modest way-fexer that he has good reason to think humbly of himself, it cannot be maintained that they contribute much to the briskness and activity of the thoroughfare, the exhilarating liveliness of which is mainly due to the pedestrians on either side of the way, and to the heavily burdened pack-horBes that move in irregularly broken lines to or from the centre of the city, which their monotonous toil helps to supply with such articles of merchandize as cannot be conveyed to town more expeditiously and cheaply on the surface of the river. Sometimes as many as six of these patient and immoderately laden animals are driven into the city from the country, like a small herd of geese, or a lot of pigs, by a single driver, who follows them at the distance of fifteen or twenty yards, well knowing that so long as he ceases to crack the whip,

---

speed was marvellous to the Oxonians who were the first to test its rapidity. It made the journey from the university to the capital in thirteen honrs :— A.D. 1669. Monday, May 2,' says Antony Wood in his autobiography, was the first day that the flying coach went from Oxon to London in one day. A. W. went in the same coach, having then a boot on each side. Among the six men that went, Mr. Rich. Holloway, a counsellor of Oxon (afterwards a judge) was one. They then (according to the Vice-Chancellor's order, stuck up in all the places) entered into the coach at the tavern door against Alls Coll. precisely at 6 o'clock in the morning, and at 7 at night they were all set down at their inn at London. The occasion of A. Wood's going to London was to carry on his studies in the Cottonian Library and elsewhere.' Such were the flying-coaches of old time which gave rise to the more modern term 'fly.'

which hangs backwards over his shoulder, none of the orderly and wearied creatures will proceed too far in advance of the others, or fail to stop at the appointed halting-place.

The gardens of Loggan's delineations, with two or three exceptions, are just Such formal, rectangular yards of pleasure-ground, as our Elizabethan forefathers were wont to lay out between the walls and the water of their moated manor-houses— spots not devoid of a certain artificial attractiveness, but chiefly remarkable for rectilineal preciseness, and for the ingenuity with which they violated every rule of natural beauty. The custodians of some of them clearly take especial pride in their fantastic specimens of topiary art; whilst others, less noticeable for the variety and grotesqueness of their devices in cut box and mutilated yew, create diversion by the intricacy and mathematical exactness of their 'plots An Oxonian garden, of the period under consideration, was never thought in a condition that would endure critical inspection until it was furnished with at least one arbour of living shrubbery, for the cultivation of meditative retirement and earwigs; and from the number of Loggan's drawings, in which a single college is provided with two or three bowers, visible from the draughtsman's point of view, one is justified in supposing that it was not unusual for a collegiate pleasure-yard to have several 'verdant grots.'

For the benefit of Oxonians, who have no copy of Loggan at hand, I may venture to speak separately of the horticultural works noticed by the artist. University College has two rectangular gardens, one of which is embellished with a grand piece of topiary ait and an enormous arbour, whilst the other is remarkable for the elaborate design of its 'plot Balliol has four geometric gardens, with three arbours, visible from the artist's point of observation. Oriel, an ill-planted but large rectangular garden, provided with a bower; and Queen's, a small garden of geometrical design. The delineator's view of New College places under observation its geometric garden and bowling-green, the latter being provided with an arbour. The chief quadrangle of Brasenose has in its middle a quaintly devised parterre, a fantastic plot, and borders of flowers. In Christ Church there appear several gardens, of geometric design, variously adorned with bowers and topiary work; and in the adjacent meadows is seen the beginning of the Broad Walk — 'Ambulacra, the Walks'—as the artist designates the avenue, with seven trees on either side. Trinity has a walled inner garden, formal, and angular, and rich in straight paths and topiary work; and a walled outer garden, laid out in the wilderness style, somewhat in accordance with the counsel of Lord Bacon, who, though he could not liberate himself altogether from the horticultural conventionalities of his period, indicated in an essay a few of the principles which the landscape-gardeners of Georgian England laid down minutely and precisely. The large open ground of St John's is divided into three gardens. Wadham has a magnificent specimen of the geometric garden, with a mound in the centre at the meeting of four cross-paths that divide the square enclosure into quarters, each of which, is subdivided into four rectangular plots; the general design and details of so remarkable a triumph of horticultural ingenuity being, no doubt, attributable to that most obliging and universally curious Dr. Wilkins who gave John Evelyn a transparent apiary. Pembroke is lavishly provided with bowers, arbour-work, and topiary extravagances; all the space of its new and larger quadrangle, and all the ground now occupied by its new buildings, being given up to ornamental gardening.

But, humble and comparatively mean though they were, the gardens of Loggan's Oxford were greatly superior to the collegiate gardens of times prior to Elizabeth's accession. It is the function of civilized woman to beautify whatever she touches, and to invest every dwelling which she makes her home with graces that are typical of her gentlest and sweetest qualities. That the university was altogether devoid of artificially arranged pleasure-grounds, or totally neglectful of horticulture, before the rise of academic womankind, I do not suggest; but there is no doubt that, during the century following the Reformation, Oxford was more indebted to the wives and daughters of her married principals than to her academic celibates for the number and considerable merit of her gardens Besides enlarging his residence for her appropriate entertainment Robert Hoveden, the first married warden of All Souls — the warden, moreover, who was so fortunate as to obtain in his twenty-seventh year the office which he held for forty-two years — gratified his wife by bringing within the boundaries of his college, and attaching to his lodge, the garden which had formerly belonged to the Rose Inn. Some hundred years later, Lady Clayton stirred Antony Wood's splenetic temper by inducing the authorities of Merton College to lay out the warden's garden afresh, purchase trees for its ornamentation, plant it with roots (some of which cost five shillings each), and provide the egregious summer-house, the cost of which amounted to one hundred pounds. And between the days of Robert Hoveden's wife and Sir Thomas Clay-ton's 'proud lady collegiate bursars were repeatedly constrained to pay bills sent in to them by gardeners retained to gratify the horticultural desires of academic gentlewomen.

Nor may it be imagined that the enclosed gardens, commemorated by Loggan's drawings, were the only grounds which imparted picturesqueness to the seat of learning. Though Christ Church and Merton meadows did not possess, till a comparatively recent date, their present opulence of noble timber, stately avenues, meandering walks, and fair lawn, they were long since rendered more charming to the eye than they would have been had they been left in natural wildness, or merely treated as so many acres of profitable pasture. When the Caroline deans caused the rubble and stone-chips, and other waste material accruing from the architectural works of the great college, to be used for the construction of sound walks in the adjacent grass-fields, they merely imitated an example which Wolsey had set them in the sixteenth century. That the Broad Walk —originally called White Walk from the colour of the materials of which it was made, and then Wide Walk when the way had become more remarkable for breadth than whiteness — was bordered by no very considerable number of trees in Charles the Second's time, Loggan intimates; but though the meads in which the Cavalier gownsmen delighted to loiter in summer, or play at leap-bar in colder seasons, were neither so well planted nor tastefully cared for as they might have been ; and though the most was not made of their natural capabilities for picturesque effect until the ' English' landscape gardeners converted them gradually into one grand and redundantly beautiful park-garden, much had been done for their adornment ere Henrietta Maria looked across them to the river from her windows in Merton.

That the Oxonians of the Caroline period did not think Christ Church meadows comparable, in respect of picturequeness, with the wildly ornamental ground lying to the rear of Magdalen College and bordered by the Cherwell, may be inferred from Antony Wood's almost total silence about the beauty of the meadows, and the enthusiasm with which he extols the unapproachable loveliness of the grove and gardens and water-walks of Waynflete's house. ' I have no more to say of this house the annalist remarks with unaccustomed fervour, ' but what may be applied to the most noble and rich structure in the learned world; that is to say, that if you have a regard to its endowment, excelleth (all things considered) any society in Europe : or to those honourable, reverend, and learned persons it hath produced, what place more ? Look upon its buildings, and the lofty pinnacles and turrets thereon, and what structure, in Oxford or elsewhere, doth more delight the eye, administering a pleasant sight to strangers at their entrance into the east part of the city ?—upon the stately tower, which containeth the most tuneable and melodious ring of bells in all these parts and beyond. Walk also into the quadrangle, and there every buttress almost of the cloister beareth an antick; into the chapel, where the eye is delighted with Scripture-history and pictures of saints in the windows, and on the east wall; into the library, and there you ll find a rare and choice collection of books, as well printed as written. Go without it, and you ?1 find it a college sweetly and pleasantly situated, whose grove and gardens, enclosed with an embattled wall by the pound, are emulous with the gardens of Hippolitus Cardinal d?ste, so much famoused and commended by Franciscus Scholtus in his *Itinerary of Italy*; go into the water-walks, and at some times in the year you will find them as delectable as the banks of Eurotas, which were shaded with bay-trees, and where Apollo himself was wont to walk and sing his lays. And of the rivers here, that pleasantly and with a murmuring noise wind and turn, may in a manner be spoken that which the people of Angoulesme in France were wont to say of their river Touvre, that " it is covered and chequered with swans, paved and floured with troutes, hemmed and bordered with cresses." Such pleasant meanders also, shadowed with trees, were there before the civil distempers broke forth, that students could not but with great delight. accost the Muses

The concluding sentence of the foregoing rhapsody seems to refer to injuries done to the umbrageous water-walks, and to imply that whilst Oxford was a Royalist garrison the military exigencies of the crisis or the barbarousness of military license diminished the attractiveness of the outer grounds of the college. That Waynfleet's house suffered grievously in its environs from the martial occupation one can readily believe, on recalling the uses to which the grounds were put by the king's artillerymen, and the necessity which existed for strongly defending so important a point. But nature soon obliterated the ravages of the war ; and long before the Latin version of Antony Wood's history saw the light, the Magdalen water-walks had recovered from whatever injuries they sustained during the civil conflict Nor has time diminished. their beauty and pleasantness, or robbed them of their ancient characteristics Oxford contains no piece, made up of architecture, plantation, paddock, shrubbery, and meandering walks, that remains more nearly what it was two or three centuries since, than the picturesque corner which the antiquarian commended with much fervour and quaintness, but no extravagance.

Like New College, the bowling-green of which society is noticed by Loggan—like Christ Church, where the aged Cranmer was permitted to play at bowls whilst his Marian persecutors were luring him to recant — and like most of the other scholastic houses, whilst bowls was as popular a pastime with clergymen and other scholars as croquet is at the present day, Magdalen had a bowling-green,—the same green over which Cromwell and Fairfax, with other generals of the Parliamentarian forces, drove the wooden spheres during the regime of the saints, and on which Addison, in time nearer the present, delighted to disport with his collegiate contemporaries. This same green was the 'Sphseristerium' which Addison celebrated in the Latin poem of sixty-six hexameters, that Dr. Ingram of Trinity erroneously attributed to Tickell, who merely edited, in 1736, the edition of his illustrious friend's mis-eellaneous works, in which the verses met the eyes of the sometimes careless author of the *Memorials of Oxford.*

The character and quality of this Addisonian tribute to a game which, though still played in oar provincial towns, has of late fallen into comparative disesteem and neglect, may be seen from the following specimen:—

' At si forte globum, qui misit, spec tat inertem
Serpere, et impressum subito languescere motum,
Pone urget sphærae vestigia, et anxius instat,
Objurgatque moras, currentique imminet orbi,

Atque ut segnis honos dextræ servetur, iniquam
Incusat terrain, ac surgentem in marmore nodum.

' Nec risus tacuere, glomus cum volvitur actus,
Infami jactu, aut nimium vestigia plumbum
Allicit, et spheeram a recto trahit insita virtus.
Tunc qui projecit, strepitus efrandit inanes,
Et, variam in speciem distorto corpore, falsos
Increpat errores, et dat convitia ligno.
Sphaera sed, irarum temnens ludibria, coeptum
' Pergit iter, nullisque movetur surda querelis.'

But though Tickell may not be credited with the ' sphseristerium he did something for Oxford's glori-fication with that imitative faculty of writing feeble verses, which he was wont to term his ' muse and which produced, together with other inconsiderable. performances, a poem on ' Queen Caroline's Rebuilding the Lodgings of the Black Prince and Henry V. at Queen's College, Oxford and the more ambitious metrical work, entitled 'Oxford and dedicated to Lord Lonsdale, in which the rhymester remarks, with a bow to his patrons,—

' Apollo smiles on Magdlen's peaceful bowers,
Perfumes the air, and paints the grot with flowers,
Where Yalden learn'd to gain the mystic crown,
And every muse was found of Addison.'

Though none of the suburban colleges (not even New College) surpassed or rivalled Magdalen in loveliness of gardens, there were two on the northern outskirts of the city—Trinity and St. John's —whose horticultural attractions were sources of boastful pride to the whole university in the earlier decades of the eighteenth century. Comprising between four and five acres, the Johnian grounds, consisting of three distinct gardens in Loggan's time, retained the principal features of their original design so late as the middle of the last century, when they contained two gardens, divided by a wall In his *Foreigner's Companion*, Salmon (1748) says of these two pleasure-grounds: 'In the first the walks are planted with Dutch elms (stunted pollards), and walks covered with evergreens: the inward garden has everything almost that can render such a place agreeable—as a terrace, a mount, a wilderness, and well-contrived arbours; but, notwithstanding, this is much more admired by strangers than the other, the outer garden is become the general rendezvous of gentlemen and ladies every Sunday in summer: here we have an opportunity of seeing the whole university to-gether almost, as well as the better sort of townsmen and ladies, who seldom fail of making their appearance here at the same time, unless the weather prevents them.' Of Trinity Gardens the same author remarks : ' The gardens of this college are large and well laid out, containing about three acres of ground They are divided into three parts; the first, which we enter from the grand quadrangle, consists of fine gravel walks and grass-plots, adorned with evergreens, and the walls entirely covered with them, as those in other college-gardens generally are. Adjoining to this, on the south, is another garden, with shady walks of Dutch elms, and beyond a wilderness, adorned with fountains, close arbours, round stone tables, and other embellishments In many particulars reminding the critical reader of the tea-gardens attached to suburban taverns (though more elegant pleasure-grounds were seldom seen at the seats of the nobility), these gardens preserved the general appearance imparted to them by their originators, until the triumph of the revolutionary landscape gardeners who, plying spade and mattock in the teeth of a derisive opposition, changed them to such places as they are now, and, it is hoped, will long remain. In the latter days of their geometrical period it was the fashion of their frequenters to attribute their angular and rectilineal characteristics to 'Dutch influence;' but at most the Hollanders and Germans did no more than add a few artificial and grotesque embellishments to the old English gardens which good taste succeeded with difficulty in banishing from the England of to-day,

CHAPTER XII

OXFORD JOKES AND SAUSAGES.

To OXONIAN humour the English language is indebted for the term ' Hocus-

Pocus,' devised by the Protestant wits of Edward the Sixth's time, to cast derision on the words ' Hoc est Corpus uttered by Catholic priests when they delivered the consecrated bread to communicants. Passing quickly from the lips of angry disputants to the general populace, the expression was adopted at the same time by practitioners of charlatanry, as a convenient phrase for implying the presence of miraculous agency, and also by the multitude, as an expression of contempt for the trickery of jugglers. Webster gives it a place in his dictionary, together with the definitions, 'a juggler, a juggler's trick, a cheat used by conjurers.'

Another colloquial pleasantry, for which Oxford may be thanked, is the proverbial expression which makes ' a dinner with Duke Humphry' synonymous with ' no dinner at all' When Humphry, Duke of Gloucester, in the middle of the fifteenth century, presented Oxford with books and money for the creation of a library—or rather, for the enlargement and restoration of a previous collection of literary treasures, and for the erection of a suitable place for their custody—the university showed proper gratitude for his grace's munificence by constituting him the Founder of the Library; and from Duke Humphry's time till the period of the seventeenth century, when Sir Thomas Bodley, by repeating on a grander scale the Duke's services to learning, may be said to have put his grace's academic nose out of joint, the Oxford University Library was no less generally known and spoken of as Duke Humphry's Library than it is now-a-days called the Bodleian Library. In those days the scholar, whose devotion to learning caused him to remain over his books in the library whilst his fellow-students were dining in their common-halls, was said to dine with Duke Humphry. Usage gave new terms and modifica-tions of meaning to the expression. The scholar, who remained in his own chamber during the dinner-hour of his college or inn, was called one of Duke Humphry's guests. And, in course of time, instead of being applicable to students who, either through inadvertence or zeal for learning, partook only of intellectual food whilst their companions were regaling themselves with substantial fare, the description was accorded to every poor bookworm or other wretch who fasted at mid-day, because he could not get together a groat and a farthing for a dinner at a cheap ordinary. It is needless to observe that there is another way of explaining the proverb ; and it is quite as needless to add that the explanation now given of Duke Humphry's fame for hospitality puts that other exposition clean out of the court of common sense.

But though the peruser of 'Oxoniana' comes every now and then on evidence that the gownsmen of old time were capable of genuine humour, I regret to say that the annals of their facetious exploits are not always provocative of the kind of laughter which wits like to occasion. Worthless they are not—for no literature which helps to illuminate the past is worthless — but the volumes, published chiefly to perpetuate the colloquial triumphs of the Oxonian ' wags' and ' smarts' of past centuries, are amongst the faintest and dullest records of human flippancy which it has been my duty to survey. In old times the lighter Oxonians were of opinion that no conversation was otherwise than sparkling which overflowed with puns, or otherwise than piquant if it was calculated to put to the blush any virtuous woman who should chance to overhear its jocular allusions to distasteful topics.

What the average pleasantries and mirth of an undergraduates' supper-party in the seventeenth century was, the reader may infer from the following account which Antony Wood gives of the 'high jinks' that caused the Mertonians of his time to roar with the boisterous glee of tipsy school-boys on the festive evenings of the winter season. At that time Christmas appearing says the annalist of doings which closed his freshman's period at Merton in 1647-8, ' there were fires of charcoal made in the Common Hall on All Saint's eve, All Saint's day and night, on the holydayes, their nights and eves between that time and Christmas day, then on Christmas eve, Christmas day, and holydayes and their nights, and on Candlemas eve, Candlemas day and night

'At all those fires every night, which began to be made a little after five of the clock, the senior undergraduate would bring into the hall the juniors or freshmen between that time and six of the clock, and there make them sit downe on a forme in the middle of the hall, joyning to the declaiming desk; which done, every one in order was to speak some pretty apothegme, or make a jest or bull, or speak some eloquent nonsense, to make the company laugh ; but if any of the freshmen came off dull, or not cleverly, some of the forward or pragmatical seniors would "tuck" them, that is, set the nail of their thumb to their chin, just under the lipp, and by the help of their other fingers under the chin, they would give him a mark, which sometimes would produce blood. On Can-dlemass Day, or before (according as Shrove Tuesday fell out) every freshman had warning given him to provide his speech, to be spoken in the public hall, before the undergraduates and servants on Shrove Tuesday night that followed, being alwaies the times for the observation of that ceremony. According to the said summons, A. Wood provided a speech as the other freshmen did. Shrove Tuesday, Feb. 15, the fire being made in the Common Hall before 5 of the clocke at night, the fellowes should go to supper before six, and making an end sooner than at other times, they left the hall to the libertie of the undergraduates, but with an admonition from one of the fellowes (who was the principal of the undergraduates and postmasters) that all things should be carried on in good order. While they were at supper in the hall, the cook (Will Noble) was making the lesser of the brass potsful of cawdel at the freshmen's charge; which, after the hall was free from the fellowes, was brought up and set before the fire in the said hall. Afterwards, every freshman, according to seniority, was to pluck off his gowne and band, and if possibly to make himself look like a scoundrell. This done, they were conducted each after the other to the high table, and there made to stand upon a forme placed thereon; from whence they were to speak their speech with an audible voice to the company; which, if well done, the person that spoke it was to have a cup of cawdle and no salted drinke; if indifferently, some cawdle and some salted drinke; but if dull, nothing was given to him but salted drinke, or salt put in college beere, with tucks to boot. Afterwards, when they were to be admitted into the fraternity, the senior cook was to administer to them an oath over an old shoe, part of which runs thus :—Item tu jurabis, quod penniless bench non visitabis, &c., the rest is forgotten, and none there are that now remembers it. After which, spoken with gravity, the freshmen kist the shoe, put on his gowne and band, and took his place among the seniors.

'Now for a diversion, and to make you laugh at the folly and simplicity of those times, I shall entertaine you with part of a speech, which A. Wood spoke, while he stood on the forme, placed on the table, with his gowne and band off and uncovered.

' "Most reverend seniors,—May it please you gravities, to admit into your presence a kitten of the muses, and a muses frog of Helicon, to croak the cataracts of his plumbeous cerebrosity before your sagacious ingenuities. Perhaps you may expect that I should thunder out demi-cannon words, and level my sulphurious throat against my fellows of the Tyrocinian crew ; but this being the universal judgment of wee freshwater Academicians, behold, as so many Stygian Furies, or ghosts risen out of their winding sheets, we present ourselves before your tribunal, and therefore I will not sublimate nor tonitruate words, nor swell into gigantick streins: such towring ebullitions do not exuberate in my Aganippe, being at the lowest ebb. I have been no chairman in the committee of Apollo's creatures, neither was I ever admitted into the cabinet councils of the Pyerian Dames, that my braines should eva-porate into high hyperboles, or that I should bastinado the times with a tart satyr of a magic pen. Indeed, I am but a freshwater soldier under the banners of Phoebus, and, therefore, cannot as yet set quart pots or double juggs in battalia, or make a good shot in sack and claret, or give fire to the pistoletto tobacco pipe, charged with its Indian powder; and, therefore, having but poor skill in such service, I were about to turne Heliconian dragooner, but as I, mounting of my dappernagg, Pegasus, behold Shrove Tuesday night arrested me, greeting me in the name of this honourable convocation, to appear before their tribunal, and make answer for my self, which, most wise seniors, shall be in this wise.

'"I am none of those may-pole-freshmen that are tall cedars before they come to be planted in the Acadamian Garden, who, fed with the papp of Aristotle at twenty or thirtie years of age, and suck at the duggs of their mother the university, the' they be high Colossus and youths rampant.

' " These are they who come newly from a baggpudding and a good brown loaf to deal with a penny-commons, as an elephant with a poor fly, tumbles it and tosses it, and at last gives him a chop, that tugg as hard for a postmaster's place as. a dog at mutton.

' " I am none of the university blood-hounds that seek for preferment, and whose noses are as acute as their eares, that lye perdue for places, and' who good saints do groan till the visitation comes. These are they that esteem a tavern as bad as purgatory, and wine more superstitious than holy water; and therefore I hope this honourable convocation will not suffer one of that tribe to taste of the sack, least they should be troubled with a vertigo and their heads turne round

' " I never came out of the country of Lapland. I am not of the number of beasts. I meane those greedie dogs and kitchen-haunters who noint their chops every night with greese, and rob the cook of his fees," &c.

' Thus he went forward with smart reflections on the rest of the freshmen and some of the servants, which might have been here set downe, had not the speech been borrowed of him by several of the seniors, who imbezzled it After he had concluded his speech he was taken down by Edmund Dickenson, one of the bachelaur-commoners of the house, who, with other bachelaurs and the senior undergraduates, made him drink a good dish of cawdle, put on his gown and band, placed him among the seniors, and gave him sack.

' This was the way and custom that had been used in the college time out of hand, to initiate the freshmen; but between that time and the restaura-tion of King Charles II. it was disused, and now such a thing is absolutely forgotten.'

Learning cannot be said to have utterly 'subdued the natural wildness and ferocity of the young gentlemen, who could find delight in listening to such a barbarous rigmarole of forced conceits, and could derive diversion from torturing freshmen of inferior brilliance, by tucking them savagely under the chin with ragged finger-nails, and compelling them to swallow doses of salt and water.

And whilst the undergraduates amused them selves with bear-play, in which the rudest schoolboys of provincial seminaries would now-a-days decline to take part, the wit of the bachelors and masters was of a decidedly primitive and uncouth kind. Too often their jests were even more discreditable to their moral than to their intellectual condition ; and when guiltless of obscenity their *jeux d esprit* consisted chiefly of obvious or antique puns, or flashes of puerile impudence. Any time between the year of the Gunpowder Plot and the last year of James the Second, it was permissible in the com-mon-rooms of the university for a graduate to tell with up-roarious glee how, when Christopher Dale, of Merton College, was hissed and hooted in con-vocation, and also on his way home from convo-cation to his own college, the witnesses of the demonstration against the unpopular magistrate remarked that he was 'proctor cum parvâ laude;'— Dale's colleague in procuratoral duty being ' little Laud who subsequently became Primate of the church and Chancellor of the university. Another favourite anecdote of the gownsmen's wine-parties in the seventeenth century commemorated the sprightliness of the bachelor of arts who, on being reproved by the Vice-Chancellor for wearing boots in defiance of the statute, which forbade academicians below the master's grade to use such costly articles of costume, raised a laugh against his censor by a retort of unapproachable effrontery and smartness. ' Sir,' said the Vice-Chancellor, 'your boots shall coat you ten groats the fine for the offence. ' I thank your worship retorted the peccant bachelor, bowing with an appropriate air of humility, 'for my shoemaker told me that they would cost me ten shillings Another academic wag, of the same century, won the applause of the schools by the promptitude with which he told a lie to the proctor who, stopping him in one of the streets of the university, asked him how he came to be out of college after nine P.M., and what it was that he carried under the sleeve of his gown. ' Sir replied the scholar, who was a servitor of Exeter College, showing the corner of a big book, whilst he concealed the flagon of beer which he was bent on conveying clandestinely into Exeter, ' my master sent me to his stationer for a copy of *Bellarmine.*' 'Very good answered the easily pacified proctor,' you may go on; your master does well to read *Bellarmine.*' The exultation of Exeter men, on hearing how the servitor had outwitted the proctor, and carried his beer in triumph into college, was equalled by the delight which so brilliant an achievement occasioned to the other houses of the university. ' Whence adds the narrator of the story, 'a bottle with a big belly is called a Bellarmine to this day, 1667

South and the clerical punsters of the Restoration period imparted to academic table-talk a spright-liness and jocosity which had not generally characterized the gossip of the halls and common-rooms during the regime of the saints : but that the collegiate standard of humour was not permanently raised by the later Cavaliers is demonstrated by the tenuity and weakness of the jokes which Nicholas Amhurst, one of the smartest Oxonians of his time, gathered into the numbers of 'Terrse Films a periodical publication, of which something must be said in another chapter.

One of the brightest and strongest of Amhurst's jocular stories relates to the keeper of an ale-house, that stood near the Oxford Pound. To call attention to his liquor the tradesman announced by placard that he sold beer by the pound, whereupon the students made a run to the place of entertainr ment to see if they could buy pudding by the yard of the tradesman who sold malt liquor by weight. Summoned to appear before the vice-chancellor and give an account of his commercial doings, the seller of beer, instead of satisfying the curiosity of his inquisitorial judge, began to spit about the vice-chancellor's parlour, to the lively astonishment and disgust of that great person, who demanded what the fellow meant by his unseemly conduct. 'You summoned me to clear myself answered the culprit, coughing and spitting still more profusely, ' and I have come to clear myself,— and I will clear myself.' 'Clear yourself, sirrah roared the vice-chancellor, 'I expect you to clear yourself in a different way from that. They tell me you sell ale by the pound.' ' No, indeed, your worship.' ' Don't you ?—then how do you ?' To which inquiry the fellow responded, 'Very well, indeed, I thank you, Mr. Vice-chancellor; pray how do you, sir ?' The impudence of this answer infuriated the vice-chancellor, who, crying out, 'Get you gone, for a rascal,' turned the taverner out of the room. ' Away went the fellow,' says Nicholas Amhurst, 'and meeting with one of the proctors, told him that the vice-chancellor desired to speak with him immediately; the proctor in great haste went to know the vice-chancellor's commands, and the fellow with him, who told the vice-chancellor, when they came before him, *that here he was. Here he is!* says the vice-chancellor. *Who is here ? Sir,* says the impudent ale-house keeper, *you bade me go for a rascal; and lo ! here I have brought you one.* But the poor fellow paid dearly for his jokes; his license was taken away, and he was committed to the castle prison.'

Mr. Amhurst's next story is no better in respect of humour, but has the merit of being shorter than the foregoing anecdote. On entering the chamber of a friend, living in Balliol College, a formal fellow of Hart Hall made a thousand scrapes and cringes, which inspired the man of Balliol to remark,' Tom, thou art just like a tree,—you are so full of your *bows*' Concerning the antecedents and subsequent fortunes of this pungent wag, Mr. Amhurst has the unkindness to be silent. Scarcely inferior, as a humourist, to the Balliol scholar, was the learned divine of Lincoln College who, on seeing an unusually large stone fitted into a church wall, remarked to a friend, Jem, that's a monstrous big stone; I wonder whether it was brought there all at once.' But this learned divine was no wit of a single *jeu d'esprit*, Equal to the emergency when he saw a young student, who was incessantly running about college, he exclaimed, 'That young fellow is the idlest fellow in the house; for every once that he goes into his room, I'11 be hanged if he does not come out of it ten times When an undergraduate of Balliol cut his throat so inexpertly that he escaped the consequences of *felo-de-se,* the principal of that learned society said to his servitor, ' Since he is not going to die, run to the buttery and sconce him five shillings, and tell him that on a repetition of the offence he shall be sconced ten shillings During the enjoyment of a moonlight night, a fellow of St John's, walking with a friend in the Johnian ' grove,' remarked, ' What fine walking is here! I wish that there was no sun, that we might walk all day long by moonlight' Speaking of ' Terra Films the series of papers from which these pleasantries have been culled, a gentleman of St. John's College, alluding to the hebdomadal character and impotent spiteftdness of the publication, observed with more truth than originality, ' 'Tis *weakly* malice.'

Another characteristic specimen of the humour of 'Terra Filius,' i.e., the humour of Augustan Oxford, is Amhurst's ' Iter Academicum: or, The Gentleman-Commoner's Matriculation:—

Being of age to play the fool,
With muckle glee I left our school
at Hoxton,
And mounted on an easy pad,
Rode with my mother and my dad
to Oxon.

' Conceited of my parts and knowledge

They enter'd me into a college, ibidem.
The master took me first aside,
Show'd me a scrawl, I read, and cry'd
Bo fidem.

' Gravely he took me by the fist,
And wished me well—we next request a tutor:
He recommends a staunch one, who
In Perkins cause had been his co-adjutor.

To see this precious stick of wood,
I went (for so they deem'd it good) in fear, sir:
And found him swallowing loyally
Six deep his bumpers, which to me seem'd queer, sir.

' He bade me sit and take my glass,
I answered, looking like an ass, I, I can't, sir.
Not drink!—you don't come here to pray !
The merry mortal said by way of answer.

'To pray, sir; no, my lad, 'tis well
Come! here's my friend, Sachererell! here's
Trappy!
Here's Ormond! Marr! in short so many
Traitors we drank, it made my cranium nappy.

' And now the company dismist,
With this same sociable priest, or fellow,
I sallied forth to deck my back
With loads of Tuft, and gown of black prunello.

' My back equipt, it was not fair,
My head should 'scape, and so as square as chess-board,

A cap I bought, my skull to screen, Of cloth without, and all within of pasteboard.

' I took my leave with many a tear
Of John our man, and parents dear, who blest me.

' The master said they might believe him,
So righteously (the Lord forgive him!) he'd govern.
He'd show me the extremest love,
Provided that I did not prove too stubborn.

' So far, so good—but now fresh foes
Began (for so the custom is) my ruin,

' Fresh foes!—with drink they knock you down,
You spoil your clothes: and your new gown.

I scarce had slept—at six—tan-tin
The bell goes—servitor comes in, gives warning.

To swear to: swore, engag'd my soul,
And paid the swearing broker whole ten shilling.

Full half a pound I paid him down,
To live in the most immoral town o' th nation:
May it ten thousand cost Lord Phyz,
For never forwarding it visitation.

It would be easy to fill a volume of moderate dimensions with jests and jocular verses, which were perpetrated by or fathered upon Oxonians, who played out their terms of frolicsome idleness in the time between Charles the Second's return from exile and the accession of the house of Hanover; but I am not aware of any essays in facetious literature attributed to youthful Oxonians of that period, which are more brilliant or pungent than the imperfectly successful exhibitions of humour which I have selected from Nicholas Amhurst's papers.

Passing over some forty years, during which the wit of the ' Terrae Filius' may be fairly regarded as representing the sportiveness of Alma Mater's more frivolous and disorderly youth, I come upon ' The Oxford Sausage; or Select Pieces. Written by the most celebrated wits of the University of Oxford. Adorned with cuts. Engraved in a New Taste, and designed by the best Masters,'—a publication which would not justify me in asserting that the Oxonian ' wags' and ' drolls' of George the Third's earlier years were much brighter and keener fellows than the ' smarts' of Amhurst's period.

One of the performances, preserved from oblivion in the 'Oxford Sausage is the following metrical advertisement which a gownsman, in whom a yearning for literary renown was combined with a strong love of mutton-pies and porter, wrote for the benefit of Benjamin Tyrrell, who, after rendering his eating-house alike popular with gownsmen, townsmen, and visitors from the country, ' formed the laudable design of obliging the university with mutton-pies twice a-week:'—

' All ye that love what's nice and rarish,
At Oxford, in St. Mary's parish,
Ben Tyrrell, cook of high renown,
To please the palates of the gown,
At three-pence each, makes mutton-pies,
Which thus he begs to advertise:
He welcomes all his friends at seven.
Each Saturday and We'n'sday even.
No relics stale, with art unjust,
Lurk in disguise beneath his crust;
His pies, to give you all fair play,
Smoak only when 'tis Market-day:
And all must own, how fresh his meat,
While Jolly's porter crowns the treat.

If rumps and kidneys can allure ye,
Ben takes upon him to assure ye,
No `cook shall better hit the taste,
For giving life and soul to paste.
If *cheap* and *good* have weight with men,
Gome, all ye youths, and sup with Ben.
If *liquor* in a mutton-pie
Has any charms, come taste and try!
0 bear me witness, Isis' sons,
Pierce but the crust—the gravy runs;
The taster licks his lips, and cries,
" 0 rare Ben Tyrrell's Mutton Pies!"
But hold—no more—I've said enough—
Or else my Pies may prove—a puff!'

Ben Tyrrell was not slow to use the puff with which the ' celebrated wit' had provided him, and on Nov. 25, 1758, he caused it to be printed in the ' Oxford Journal.,

Whilst Ben Tyrrell's mutton-pies gratified the discriminating but not fastidious palates of Oxonian gourmands, Mrs. Spreadbury was at the head of the sausage business, and Captain Jolly won the applause of undergraduates by lowering the price of his porter from sixpence to fourpence a quart *pro bono publico* as the editor of' The Oxford Sausage' playfully remarks in a note of characteristic learning and elegance. Rendering due honour to Spreadbury and Jolly, whilst he extols the first pieman of his age, one of the celebrated wits, modestly concealing himself under the *nam de plume* of *Utoptkoc* dis-burthens his full soul in the following style:—

' I'd raise thy' (*i.e.* Tyrrell's) culinary fame
Above immortal Spreadbury's name;
Though from all cooks, a matron wise,
In sausages she bore the prize:

Her seasoning hand should yield to thine,
Thy mutton should her pork outshine.
Nor shall the muse esteem it folly
To blend with thine the praise of Jolly,
Thy lov'd compeer! congenial friend!
Who mild, when evening shades descend,
Imparts the froth-crowned porter's aid,
To smooth the serious brow of Trade ;
Both shall together mount the skies,
The porter his—but thine the pies.
Thine is the House, dear Ben, to call at,
Or for the pocket or the palate,
For thee the citizens and cit
Their cold boiled leg and carrots quit;
Grave aldermen, ambitious, share
In Alma Mater's classic fare;
The blooming toasts of Oxford town
Catch the contagion of the Gown,
And wish the wonted evening nigh,
To have a finger in the pie !'

Contemporary with Ben Tyrrell was the pie-woman, Nell Batchelor, whose seasonable death, after a long career of professional labours and sus-cesses, so wrought upon the feelings of one of her patrons that he took pen in hand and produced for her grave the following epitaph, alike remarkable for affectionateness to the deceased lady and respect for the feelings of her survivors:—

' Here deep in the dust The mouldy old crust
Of Nell Batchelor lately was shoven,
Who was skill'd in the arts
Of pies, puddings, and tarts,
And knew every use of the oven.

' When she'd lived long enough,
She made her last puff.
A puff by her husband much praised:
Now here she doth lye,
And makes a dirt-pye
In hopes that her dust will be raised.'

Other Oxonian worthies of a century or more since—such as Blagrave the job-master, and Messrs. Glass and Nourse, the surgeons,—are commemorated by the contributors to "The Oxford Sausage the ingredients of which miscellaneous dish comprise materials more likely to offend than gratify the palate of this fastidious age. But though a little of the 'Sausage' is quite enough, and to reproduce much of it in these pages would lead to a rupture between their author and his customary readers, the work is noteworthy for the light which it throws on the social ways and tone of the university in days when gownsmen, living under the restraints of collegiate discipline, and possessing all the aids towards virtuous living of which the collegiate system is supposed to be productive, drank far more beer than was good for them, smoked inordinately, ate mutton-pies voraciously, and made love to barmaids without losing the respect of their comrades.

CHAPTER XIII

TERRÆ FILII.

GIVING a definition by no means deficient in justice, though it requires explanatory comment, John Evelyn described a terræ-filius, *as an university buffoon. What the court fool was in the sovereign's chamber of audience, what the anti-mask of beggars and cripples in a feudal pageant, what the late Colonel Sibthorp in the House of Commons, the* terræ-filius was at the ceremonious celebrations of the Oxford Act. The comic feature of a grave entertainment, he was retained to enliven with verbal antics the proceedings which, however much they might redound to the dignity of learning, were apt to prove wearisome to auditors who could not understand Latin, and were not initiated in the philosophical jargon of the schools.

Like the prevaricator of a Cambridge commence-ment, he was appointed to discharge the functions of an academic Merry-Andrew. Much of the fun of the formal disputations depended on his quickness in turning to ridicule the general purport or exceptional absurdities of the serious speeches, and on his ability to mimic whatever was grotesque in the oratorical manner of opponents, respondents, and moderators. Though he was forbidden to put an actual stop to the argumentations by incessant loquacity, he might break in upon them at any moment with humorous rejoinder, ironical applause, or droll suggestion; and in the intervals between the bursts of controversy—whilst the disputants were recovering wind and temper, or whilst a fresh lot of intellectual gladiators armed themselves for fight—he gave reins to his malicious talkativeness, and made the house roar with laughter by chaffing the grandest dignitaries of the university, and calling them to account for whatever offences they had committed, since the previous Act, against com-mon sense or good morals. But whilst he enjoyed the privileges of an official jester, and, like the slaves during the Roman saturnalia, might speak his mind with considerable freedom about his superiors, there were limits of toleration which his sportive impudence could not exceed with immunity from punishment. The court fool, who carried his foolery beyond the bounds of customary license, was liable to be called to order with whip-cord. The terræ-filius, guilty of the same indiscretion, was sometimes kicked out of St. Mary's Church, and taught by the flagellator of the schools to laugh on the wrong side of his mouth.

Like the Cambridge prevaricators, the terræ-filius of Oxford sometimes worked in couples, but though it was usual for an Act to be enlivened by two mountebanks, who talked up to each other's pre-arranged jests, and kept the ball of satire rolling from one side of the theatre to the other, it often happened that a single jester, through inability to find a congenial comrade, played the fool's game without assistance. Indeed there are grounds for the opinion that originally the labour of imparting jocularity to the proceedings of the Act invariably devolved on a single buffoon, and that the appearance of a second terræ-filius on the stage was an innovation upon the ancient usage of the scholars.

But so much uncertainty covers the early history of terræ-filii, *that I should not like to give a positive opinion on this point. That the* terræ-filius *had a recognized official position, and was no mere creature of the unrecognized license of the junior members of university, is, however, certain. The senior proctor sanctioned his proceedings at each Act, by formally appointing him to his occasionally perilous office; and when he had become an intolerable nuisance, it was found impossible to suppress him until Convocation had been regularly called upon to vote that an end should be put to his existence.*

The politico-religious disturbances of the Reform-ation period gave such prominence and importance to the jests of the terræ-filii that their existence has been erroneously said to have originated in the times when religious innovators encouraged subordinate persons to exhibit contempt for their official superiors. Speaking of the academic mountebanks, Ayliffe observes : ' This manner of sportive wit had its origin at the time of the Reformation, when the gross absurdities and superstitions of the Romish Church were to be exposed, and should have been restrained to things, and not have reached men's persons and characters; yet it has since become very scandalous and abusive, and in nowise to be tolerated in an university, where nothing might appear but religion, learning, and good manners.'

But though the origin of the terræ-filii *must be sought for in times long prior to the Reformation, the academic jesters are far less conspicuous in the annals of Catholic Oxford than in the records which make up the history of the university from Elizabeth's accession to William the Third's arrival in England. In 1591 John Hoskyns, who subsequently attached himself to Sir Walter Raleigh, and assisted that gallant scholar in producing the* History of the World, *came to signal grief through the indiscretions which he committed whilst officiating as* terræ-filius, *after he had taken his master's degree. For satirical utterances, exceeding the license of his office, this most unfortunate of scholastic buffoons was deprived of his fellowship in New College, expelled from the university, and thrown upon the world to sustain himself as he best could by the wit which he had exhibited so offensively to the Oxonian authorities. Another* terræ-filius, *who had cause to rue the day when vanity inspired him to don the jester's belled cap* and turn his betters to ridicule, was Mr. Masters, who in 1638, when Oxonian dons were unusually disposed to severity, and bestirred themselves to maintain academic discipline by rigid enforcement of the Caroline code, was banished from Oxford on account of his slanderous reflections on divers heads of houses.

During the regime of saints the Oxonian terræ-filii distingushed themselves by the sauciness and levity of their tirades against the more austere and vexatious disciplinarians. That the university during the Commonwealth cherished a considerable number of students, who equalled or surpassed the scholars of less severe times in frivolity and disorderliness, and that many of the gownsmen of the same period were at no pains to conceal their devotion to the exiled Stuarts and their detestation of Cromwell's government, I have remarked in a former chapter. The reader, therefore, will learn, without surprise, that whilst' the blessed saints' were in power, no public Act was celebrated in the schools without more or less scandalous exhibitions of the hostility with which the Royalist scholars regarded the Evangelical divines, and the other representatives of the usurper's authority. Alike in 1651, on the occasion of the first Act celebrated after the Parliamentarian visitation of the college—in 1655, when another Act was kept after three years' discontinuance of the ancient celebrations—and in 1658, shortly before Oliver Cromwell's death, the terræ-filii were guilty of excesses of impudence that provoked the disapprobation of auditors, who were bound neither by affection nor interest to the persons against whose fame and dignity the buffoons directed their keenest satire.

In the first of these three Acts, Thomas Careless, of Balliol College, and William Leving, of St. John's, were the spokesmen of the godless and malcontent section of the university. At the second, folly and satire were represented by our old friend, Robert Whitehall, who, after making his peace with the Puritans, retained so much of his Cavalier spirit and ' malignant' humour, that he seized the opportunity to deride the discipline to which prudential considerations had induced him to submit. Whitehall's coadjutor was John Glendall, M.A., of Brasenose, of whom Wood tells us, ' He was a great mimic, and acted well in several plays, which the scholars acted by stealth, either in the stone-house behind, or southward from Pembroke College, or in Kettle Hall, or at Halywell Mill, or in the Refectory at Gloucester Hall

A. Wood was well acquainted with him, and delighted in his company The terræ-filii *at the last Act celebrated during Oliver Cromwell's chancellorship were Thomas Pittie, first of Trinity, and subsequently of Lincoln, whose* terræ-filial speech gave the Precisians such offence that they expelled him from the university, and Lancelot Addison, in after-time Dean of Lichfield and father of the essayist, who, sharing in the offence of his comrade, but, escaping with a lighter punishment, was permitted to remain in the university, on making a public recantation of the more scandalous of his satirical utterances, and expressing contrition for all the witty things that he had said in contempt of devout' dons

Besides the tumultuous disorder that resulted from the comic extravagances of Robert Whitehall and John Glendall, the Public Act of 1655 witnessed a riot, which, though it may have been aggravated by those wanton speakers, had its origin in a misadventure for which the terræ-filii were not accountable. 'As there had not been an Act solemnized for several years/ says the annalist, ' it was such a novelty to the students of the university, that there was great rudeness committed both by them and by the concourse of people who attended, in getting into places and thrusting out strangers, during the time of that solemnity. Whereupon the vice-chancellor, Dr. Greenwood, of Brasenose, a severe and choleric governor, was forced to get several guards of musketeers out of the Parliament garrison then in Oxford, to keep all the doors and avenues, and to let nobody in, except those whom the vice-chancellor and his deputies appointed. There was then great quarrelling between scholars and soldiers, and thereupon blows and bloody noses followed.'

How warmly some of the authorities resented the reflections cast upon them by the terræ-filii *of 1658, was manifested by the futile measures which they took for the extinction of a usage which, however harmless it may have been in earlier times, had for the greater part of a century been far more productive of scholastic animosities than of innocent diversion. ' In a Convocation then held says Antony Wood, under date July 30, 1658, 'it was proposed by the vice-chancellor, that the* terræ-filii (whose office was now accounted scandalous to the university and such that styled themselves godly) should be taken away. Upon which proposal, the House seeming generally to cry " Non," he required the masters to divide, viz., those that were for the terræ-filii *to go to one side of the House, and those against them to the other, supposing thereby that no sober man would appear to the face of the House for them. But some of the masters thereupon calling for a scrutiny and others making a ridiculous matter of it, the vice-chancellor was in a manner forced to sit down, and meddle no more in the matter. The occasion of it was, 1. That the* terræ-fiilii, *for some years before this, did not only not spare to tell, in their respective speeches, some of the doctors their crimes, but also to let fall various expressions that seemed to the godly to be profane and obscene. 2. The speech of Lancelot Addison, of Queen's College (this or the year before), one of the* terrce-jilii, *which, giving very great offence, he was forced to recant in the Convocation on his knees; and glad he was that he could escape with no greater punishment 3. The various reflections in speeches, sermons, common discourses, &c, made by the said godly party against them, but, above all, that speech delivered by the Greek Professor, Oct. 14, 1657, which, though then with the author, was made very ridiculous by the juniors (who took him for no other than a time-serving orator), yet, when 'twas published, gave great content to the seniors (especially the godly), and did provoke them the more to take away and destroy that office/*

Belonging to the order of brilliant young men, who are more eager for the applause of their youthful comrades than for the approbation of men of maturer years, and whom prudence seldom restrains from giving offence to the powerful so long as they can win the admiration of the frivolous, the terrce-filii seldom followed up the social successes of their student-days by achieving eminence in the learned professions. I am not aware that any terræ-filius *rose to be a bishop, or judge, or political leader, or commercial magnate. Many of them became notorious 'black sheep;' and I doubt not that if we could recover the personal stories of all the gay and disorderly young gentlemen, who were the successive buffoons of the university of the seventeenth century, the majority of them would be found to have died of disappointment, penury, and bad liquor, at the early period of life when 'fast men pay the ordinary penalties of excess. But though the general fate of* 'terræ-filii was miserable, biography mentions a few notable men, who, after figuring as the official jesters of Public Acts, became respectable and prosperous, though not eminently fortunate, members of society. Of one of these exceptions—Lancelot Addison, of Queen's—mention has already been made. In the list, also, of university buffoons, whose levity did not bring them to ruin, a place may, perhaps, be assigned to South, whose abilities and learning would, doubtless, have raised him to the highest preferments of the Church, had his reputation for discretion and devoutness equalled his wit and oratorical proficiency. That he ever discharged the functions of a terræ-filius *in St Mary's Church I am not aware; but the author of 'Oxoniana' records that a* 'terræ-filius speech written by the celebrated Dr. South' was preserved in the Bodleian Library, a composition of which, by the way, the collector remarks, It is very deficient in wit, and its topicks are low and vulgar

Though the Royalists returned to Oxford in 1660 with no disposition to muzzle the terræ-filii, *and were infinitely delighted with their raillery so long as they were content to deride the Puritans, the scientific innovators of the Royal Society, and other persons whom Oxonians of the old school regarded with hostility and suspicion, the cry was soon again heard that the licentious speeches of the privileged jesters were injurious to discipline, hurtful to manners, and intolerably prejudicial to the fame of honest people. Per-sisting in their comparatively recent course of reviewing censoriously the private ways and personal peculiarities of the principal personages of the university, the caustic orators proceeded to excesses of irreverence and slanderous scurrility that were alike offensive to decency and truth. Combining the vices of Whitehall courtiers with the unrefined pleasures of roystering rural gentry, the life of Charles the Second's Oxford teemed with abuses and scandals, which the buffoons turned to account with characteristic smartness and malevolence. The* terræ-filius would convulse his auditors at a Public Act by calling to a reverend doctor, notorious for his fondness of high play, and asking him in a significant voice where he bought his loaded dice. The laughter occasioned by this sally having subsided, the jester, after restoring to his pocket the dice-box which he had rattled in his victim's face, would turn upon another ecclesiastical dignitary, and warn him never again to kiss his neighbour's wife in a summer-house that could be overlooked by the undergraduates of his own college. The especial failing of a third ruler of a scholastic house would be lashed in a burlesque homily that one of the terrce-filii would deliver against drunk-ards in high place.

Had the jesters directed their satire at none but flagrant offenders, it is probable that no voice would have been raised to denounce their licen-tiousnesa Had the satirical representations been truthful in the main, and innocent of language calculated to put women to the blush, the culprits would scarcely have dared to exclaim against an exposure which was due to their misconduct, and likely to deter others from following their evil examples But not content with whipping notorious misdemeanants, the comic censors, adopting the rumours and gossip of the common-rooms as substantial and unimpeachable evidence, preferred publie charges of immorality against principals and tutors who had been guilty of nothing worse than trivial indiscretions. Occasionally, it happened that men were held up to social opprobrium for offences of which they were utterly incapable. Nor were gownsmen, of stainless lives and honourable years, the only sufferers from the reckless calumniousness of the sportive censors, who sometimes exhibited no more respect for feminine weakness than reverend age.

On the occasion of the opening of the Shel-donian Theatre, in 1669, John Evelyn was so disgusted at the grossness and scurrility of a terræ-filius, *that he urged the Vice-Chancellor to take measures against the repetition of so scandalous a performance. That Archbishop Sheldon's niece, Catherine, suffered from the imputations put upon her by another* terræ-filius, *after she had become a prelate's wife, we know from an entry in Pepys' diary. For reflecting indecently on Sir Thomas Spencer's friendly intercourse with a lady of condition, More, of Merton, one of the terrce-filii in 1681, was soundly and properly thrashed, on leaving the theatre, by one of the natural guardians of the gentlewoman's honour. At other times the* terræ-filii, *avoiding offences which rendered them liable to expulsion or horsewhipping, roused ill-blood amongst the students by railing at each other's colleges. For instance, in 1682, when Mr. Bowles, of New College, and Mr. James Allestree, of Christ Church, were the* terræ-filii, *the New College man abused Christ Church, whilst the* terræ-filius *of Christ Church retorted by speaking ill of New College. That the terrce-filial speeches underwent no change for the better in the earlier years of the eighteenth century, in which age they were eventually discontinued after many vain attempts to preserve the fun, without perpetuating the malignity, of the ancient practice, may be inferred from the note in Dr. Rawlinson's MS. diary, quoted by the author of 'Oxoniana,' 'Oct. 3, 1713, Dr. Gardiner chosen Vice-Chan-cellor again the third time for the year ensuing. At the same time a libel called a speech, that was intended to have been spoken by a* terræ-filius, *was by order of the Convocation burnt by the hands of the common bedel in the theatre yard'*

What the average speech of a terræ-filius *was at this date the reader may learn from the explanatory statement of Bloom, the* terræ-filius *of the* Act at Oxford — a comedy of which we spoke in a previous chapter as having been put on the stage of Drury Lane, 1704-6. 'You expect says the character of the comedy, 'a great deal, and you will have very little: that is, little wit, for the sake of the grave dons; less scandal, for that of the ladies; and no Latin, to oblige the beau-students.

'A terræ-filius uses to abuse everybody—but himself, unless you 1l say he abuses himself most in being a terræ-filius; *for he must either be superlatively impudent, and so expelled, or em-phatically dull, and condemned to the university* utrum horum, — chuse you whether. Why, faith, 1'11 be both — in a different way. A young man should be impudent in private, to recommend him to the ladies, and very dull in public, to qualify him for preferment.

To begin, then, with as little method as my predecessors, 1'11 first acquaint you what a terræ-filius is ; why, he's the university's jester, the terror of fuddling doctors and dissolute commoners, a servitor in scandal, and harlequin of the sciences. He has the modesty of an informer, the manners of a Dutch trooper, the learning of a mountebank, and the wit of a projector, who obliges the publick and perfects his own ruin. His continual railing at the University looks as if he were married to her, and his expulsion proves that he is divorc'd from her.

" He aims at wit, and loses fame,
Secures contempt, attempting at a name."

And now, pray, what is a *terrae-filius's* speech? Why, 'tis an anti-panegyrick, where as much pains is taken to detract as in the other to flatter; 'tis the reverse of a funeral sermon, where the whole care is to bespatter the living, as that is to bedaub the dead; 'tis an incongruous medley of flash, invective, grimace, and front—a sort of law-oratory without truth or modesty; 'tis generally made by a club, consequently good for nothing; therefore 'tis like a confederacy, where they all rely upon one another, and nothing's done.'

When the terræ-filius had thus become the witless mouthpiece of a club of scandalmongers and angry politicians, who used him as an instrument for scattering calumnies which they had the baseness to invent, whilst lacking the courage to utter them with their own lips, the proper time had come for terminating his inglorious career. But, unfortunately for the peace of the university and Alma Mater's reputation in the country, the long line of terræ-filii was not closed until the buffoons had for many years persisted in their scandalous violations of justice and decency.

CHAPTER XIV

THE CONSTITUTION CLUB.

THOUGH the indignation occasioned in the university and throughout the country by James the Second's illegal proceedings at Oxford was largely accountable for the Revolution of 1688, and though the resistance which he encountered from the Oxonian authorities was one of the chief political forces which drove the obstinate monarch from his throne, the change of dynasty was no sooner accomplished than the doctrines of divine right and non-resistance were proclaimed more vehemently than ever from the pulpit of St. Mary's by preachers, whose utterances were designed to throw discredit on the result of the recent disturbances. In so far as she had appeared to concur with the revolutionists who had expelled James and welcomed William, Oxford, it was maintained, had never relinquished the sacred principles which demonstrated the absolute unlawfulness of rebellion. She had never exceeded the bounds of dutiful remonstrance and affectionate expostulation. For the good of the nation and its divinely commissioned owner, she had protested, but had never resisted. The manner in which the king had exercised his indefeasible right to do what he liked with his own had, no doubt, occasioned Alma Mater serious anxiety; but she was innocent of rebellious intention. The exiled James was her lawful sovereign; and her loyal sons would never, during his life, cease to pray for his restoration, and after his death would persist in their allegiance to the lawful heir of his throne.

Such were the spirit and language of the majority of Oxonians on the arrival of William of Orange, and such they remained when the usurper, as the Jacobites designated him, paid Oxford the brief visit concerning which Evelyn wrote in his diary under date September 29, 1695,—' The King went a progress into the north, to show himself to the people against the elections, and was everywhere complimented, except at Oxford, where it was not as he had expected, so that he hardly stopped an hour there, and, having seen the theatre, did not receive the banquet proposed.' And many a year passed ere the university ceased to be the chief home and rallying point of the Jacobites, who plotted to bring about a second Restoration, When the Hanoverian dynasty was beset with secret enemies and open foes, and stood in urgent need of a larger measure of patriotic support from the nobility and gentry, its hottest and most dangerous enemies were men of Oxford education, or men who enjoyed the warmest confidence of the rulers of the university. Cambridge favoured Whig principles; but Oxford persevered in her Jacobitical Toryism, so long as the faintest possibility of success remained to the Jacobite cause. When the Hanoverian sovereign gratified the Cantabrigian Whigs with a present of books, he despatched a troop of horse to overawe the students of Jacobite Oxford,—presents which elicited the well-known epigram from an Oxford wit:—

' Our gracious monarch view'd with equal eye
The wants of either university.
Troops he to Oxford sent, well knowing why,
That learned body wanted loyalty.
But books to Cambridge sent, as well discerning,
That that right loyal body wanted learning.'

Had these lines provoked no retort from the sister university, Oxford would for many a day have exulted in their pleasant humour and piquant malice : but unfortunately for the Jacobite scholars, they had scarcely had their first laugh out, when a Cantabrigian retaliated, with finer finish and keener point:—

'Our king to Oxford sent a troop of horse,
For Tories own no argument but force,
With equal care to Cambridge books he sent,
For Whigs allow no force but argument.'

Without denying merit to the epigram which provoked the telling reply, even Oxonian readers of these Annals must admit that from this contest of raillery Oxford came off second-best

But even in the times when Jacobite Toryism prevailed most strongly at Oxford, the university comprised a small minority of Whigs, who were per-mitted to reside in the college without molestation, or at least without grievous persecution, so long as they kept their opinions to themselves, and forbore to annoy their powerful adversaries. In the Tory days of Queen Anne, when the Jacobite high-churchmen had nearly everything that they desired in the way of political influence and religious patronage, comparative harmony existed between Alma Mater's many Tories and the few Whigs. Whilst the former were jubilant, the latter refrained from action calculated to irritate their rivals. But so soon as the Whigs rose to supremacy together with George the First, and the Jacobites appealed to their king-over-the-water for liberation from Hanoverian thraldom, the feud betwixt the 'ins' and the 'outs' raged more furiously at Oxford than in any other city of the kingdom.

At this crisis, 'New and 'Oriel' were the chief quarters of the few Oxonian Whigs, who had the courage to proclaim their attachment to the House of Hanover, and their abhorrence of proceedings that aimed at revival of the Stuart dynasty in the person of the Pretender. Prominent amongst the Whigs of New College were five Fellows: Henry Thomas, MA., Carew Reynell, Sir William Holford, Paul Bearcroft, B.A., and Edward Thompson; the Rev. George Lavington, M.A., chaplain; and four gentlemen-commoners, Richard Wykeham, William Moss, Andrew Corbet, and William Wharton. In Oriel College Whig principles were represented by

Messrs. Hamilton, Yeoman, Harle, Hales, Hadley, Francis Burton, Sayer, Charles Ingram, the last-named of whom was a gentleman-commoner. The Honourable Charles Compton, Sir William Stapleton, Bart, and Mr. Fox of Christ Church were Whigs. The Honourable Mr. Yelverton, of Hart Hall, was an enthusiastic supporter of King George, and abhorred the Pretender. The same was the case with Sir Henry Hoo Keates, Bart, of Worcester College, Barzillai Jones, LL.B., Fellow of All Souls', Mr. Gharnock, gentleman-commoner of Merton, Mr. John Maynard, gentleman-commoner of St John's, Mr. Lister, B.A., of Trinity, and Mr. Sutton, gentleman-commoner of Wadham.

Having formed themselves into a political club, called the Constitution Club, these gentlemen de-clared that they would liberate loyal Oxonians from the insolent despotism of the Jacobites, who had for years been paramount in the university, and were then busy in sowing disaffection to the king in the minds of undergraduates. The King's Head Tavern, in High Street, was the house where the Constitutionalists met to drink punch to King George's prosperity, and deliver themselves of anti-Jacobite sentiments: and on May 28, 1715,—not May, 1714, as the author of the ' Terrae-Filius' papers erroneously represents—there occurred between the members of the club on the one hand, and the Tory gownsmen on the other, such a row as Oxford had not witnessed for several years.

The Constitutionalists had raised before their hotel a pile of materials for a bonfire, in which it was their intention to burn an effigy of the deceased queen; and they were sitting over their liquor and talk, waiting for the arrival of dusk, when a numerous assemblage of Tory collegians and several rioters of the lowest riff-raff of the city, made a rush at the stack of combustibles, and bore off the logs and faggots. Other Jacobite gownsmen threw money to the rabble from the windows of houses adjoining the tavern, and incited the mob to violent action, by crying aloud, ' Down with the Constitutioners,' ' Down with the Whigs,' No George, James for ever/ Catching up the cries, the rabble cheered the Pretender, Ormond, Bolingbroke, and lost no time in giving expression to their politico-religious convictions, by attacking a Presbyterian meeting-house, gutting it, demolishing part of its outer walls, and burning its pulpit in the public way, near Carfax. The clerk—or Amenraiser, as he was termed—of the conventicle tried to save the pulpit from the flames, and for his pains was set in the stocks by the rioters. On receiving intelligence of the disturbance, the senior proctor hastened to the King's Head, and dispersed the club; whereupon the Hanoverian partisans retired to their colleges, contributing on their way to the general commotion, by letting off fire-arms in the streets. After reaching his rooms in Hart Hall, Mr. Yelverton fired his gun several times from his window that opened into the thoroughfare ; and at a later hour, some of the rioters on running past Oriel were shot at by fortunately bad marksmen from the windows of the college.

Towards the close of the following day the riot was renewed A Quakers' chapel and the private house of a peaceful Friend were attacked and stripped of their furniture by a mob of roaring blackguards, who, seizing the opportunity for a row, sided with the anti-Constitutionalists of the university. That this singular coalition, between the scum of the city and the Jacobites of the colleges, was brought about by bribery cannot be proved, but the members of the Constitution Club maintained that their collegiate adversaries paid the mob for its scandalous co-operation. The impartial reader, however, declines to believe that either party of the gownsmen was innocent of turbulent excess. Anyhow, the disturbance was a brisk and somewhat alarming affair, and justified the apprehensions with which it was regarded by the eyewitness who wrote, 'After these burnings were finished, and the mob dispersed, a party came down by Oriel College, where one Mr. Charles Ing—m, brother of Lord Tr—m, having collected a great number of his own party into a room, which they called the Guard-Room, and which was replenished with guns, pistols, powder, and ball, which they made sufficient use of, without any pro-vocation. As soon as the people came near the college, the fire-arms were immediately discharged, and a person wounded in the groin, which gave just grounds to the injured mob, to demand justice; this was required at the college-gate, but denied; and had not the Provost and Fellows come down, and one of the people interposed, till justice was promised on the offenders, the college might have been pulled to the ground, and the people De-Witted. Thus ended this troublesome night, not without great joy to the Constitution Club.'

Like the more obstinate and disastrous riots of mediaeval Oxford, this disturbance, after occasioning angry discussion and bootless inquiry in schools and courthouses, was allowed to pass without correction, as an affair the blame of which attached to so many persons, whom it would be unwise to punish according to their deserts, that policy recommended an extension of forgiveness to every one concerned in it. But though just nothing came of the proceedings in the Vice-Chancellor's court against the turbulent gownsmen and at the assizes against the laical rioters, the magnates of the university did not readily cease to preach against the Constitutionalists, whom they charged in sermons, scholastic lectures, and private discourse, with malice and untruth. Far from being more loyal to the new king than other gownsmen it was averred that the Constitutioners, whilst' shrouding themselves under the specious name of the Constitution Club, were enemies to monarchy and all good government, and had been the authors of all tumults and disorders that had happened in the city or county of Oxford.' Nicholas Amhurst says a good deal in the way of ridicule and wrath about the slanderous virulence with which the academic authorities spoke of the Whig gownsmen. The most scurrilous reflections on them says the angry pamphleteer, ' were constantly thrown out in the lent verses, sermons, declamations, and all other public exercises. Even those graver tools, the Vice-Chancellor and proctors, to enliven their dull harangues, and gain the applause of the subordinate rabble, never failed, in their most solemn speeches before the Convocation, to fall foul and heavy on the Constitution Club. One of the proctors in particular had the modesty and good manners to tell the Convocation, that the Constitutioners were, "Homunciones nequissimi, diis hominibusque invisi," i.e. most vile wretches, who were hated by gods and men. At the same time that this crea-ture had the impudence to prate thus, it was known to the whole university, that a marquis, several noblemen's sons, two or three baronets, besides a great number of clergymen, and others of the best rank and quality, were members of the Constitution Club. But all the base and scandalous methods that had been practised by the university against the Constitutioners, was not able to discourage those gentlemen from adhering to their duty, and manifesting a proper zeal for the honour and interest of his Majesty on every occasion. They still con-tinued their weekly meeting; and instead of being weakened by opposition, they grew stronger by it, and increased the more in number. And as their number increased, so did the malice and resentment of their enemies, whose thoughts were wholly bent upon revenge, and upon contriving methods to extirpate the club.

On the 29th of May, in the year after this riot, the Constitution Club again came into collision with academic authority, under circumstances that occasioned the proctors several days of perplexity, and caused Mr. Meadowcourt, of Merton, a much longer term of annoyance.

In the evening of that day the Constitutioners were at their tavern, drinking with certain officers of Colonel Handyside's regiment—quartered at Oxford for the express purpose of keeping the Jacobite gownsmen in order—when a mob gathered before the King's Head, and insulted the club with hisses and denunciations. The Tory gownsmen screamed at the top of their voices, 'Down with the Roundheads!' and amidst the cheers of the laical riff-raff some of the vociferous gentlemen flung squibs and crackers through the open windows of the club upon the table of the convivial adherents of the House of Hanover.

The commotion was momentarily growing more threatening, when at eleven P. M. the sub-proctor (Mr. Holt, of Magdalen College) entered the club-room, and, addressing Mr. Meadowcourt, the president of the evening, asked how it came that in violation of two chief rules of academic discipline the gownsmen present were holding a convivial meeting in a tavern, and were absent from their college after nine o'clock P.M. Though he had spent several hours in drinking copiously to King George's success in life, the president was equal to the emergency. 'Sir he answered with a deferential bow to the magistrate, 'we are commemorating the restoration of Charles the Second, of blessed memory, and drinking King George's health; and you will greatly oblige us if you unite with us in rendering honour to our virtuous sovereign, and drink a bumper to his prosperity, and to the confusion of his enemies.'

Mr. Holt found himself in an awkward position at a time when toast-drinking was still in the full tyranny of fashion, and the most courteous refusal of a toast was a declaration of contempt for the person pledged. If he drank the proffered glass, he would become an accomplice and participator in the orgy. On the other hand, by declining to drink the toast he would render himself liable to charges of disaffection and flagrant disloyalty to his liege lord. He hesitated betwixt the two horns of the dilemma. ' Sir,' urged the excellent Mr. Meadow-court, pointing to the standing gownsmen who had risen on their sub-proctor's appearance, and to the military officers who had resumed their seats after rendering the ordinary demonstration of courtesy to the intruder, 'surely in the presence of the loyal scholars of our university, and before these gentlemen of the sword, each of whom holds a commission from his Majesty, you will not decline to join with us in praying, " God save the King."

Seizing the glass which Mr. Meadowcourt had filled for his victim, Mr. Holt said, ' To the King! God bless him! and may he long reign over us!' and then tossed the liquor down his throat before he retreated from the scene of his discomfiture. The regulation number of hurrahs followed the toast; and when the sovereign had received the musical honours due to his benevolent joviality, the crestfallen Mr. Holt was attended to the door of the tavern by one of Handyside's captains, who in a husky voice assured the magistrate that he would look after the youngsters, who were an 'uncomly jollian taining lot o' flers

After night comes the morning, and it is almost needless to observe that on the morning of May 30, 1716, Mr. Meadowcourt ascertained that authority was not disposed to see the fun, and nothing more, of his last night's frolic.

In due course there appeared in the Black Book, 'that dreadful and gloomy volume,' as Nicholas Amhurst calls it a Latin entry, of which the following is the English version:—

' Let Mr. Carty, of University College, be kept from the degree which he stands next for, for the space of one whole year.

'I. For profaning, with mad intemperance, that day, on which he ought, with sober cheerfulness, to have commemorated the restoration of Charles II. and the royal family, nay, of monarchy itself, and the Church of England.

'II. For drinking in company with those persons who insolently boast of their loyalty to King George, and endeavour to render almost all the university, besides themselves, suspected of disaffection.

' III. For calling together a great mob of people, as if to see a show, and drinking impious execrations out of the tavern-window against several worthy persons, who are the best friends to the Church and the king, by this means provoking the beholders to return them the same abuse, from whence followed a detestable breach of the peace.

' IV. For refusing to go home to his college after nine o'clock at night, though he was more than once commanded to do it by the junior proctor, who came thither to quell the riot.

' V. For being catched at the same place again by the senior proctor, and pretending, as he was admonished by him, to go home; but with a design to come and drink again.

' Let Mr. Meadoweourt, of Merton College, be kept back from the degree which he stands for next, for the space of two years; nor be admitted to supplicate for his grace until he confesses his manifold crimes, and asks pardon *upon his knees* .

VI. Not only for being an accomplice with Mr. Carty in all his faults (or rather crimes), but also:

' VII For being not only a companion, but likewise a remarkable abettor of certain officers, who ran up and down the High Street with their swords drawn, to the great terror of the townsmen and scholars.

' VIII. For breaking out to that degree of im-pudence (when the proctor admonished him to go home from the tavern at an unseasonable hour) as to command all the company, with a loud voice, to drink King George's health.

' JOH. W., Proc. jun.

When two years had elapsed, the culprit was not permitted to proceed at once to his degree. The vice-chancellor, proctors, and Messrs. White (the junior proctor in 1716), and Holt (the sub-proctor who had been foreed to drink the king's health), sent him to and fro for several months, vainly soliciting each of his enemies by turn that he might be no longer hindered from taking his degree. Part of his sentence was that he should ' ask pardon on his knees;' and though the authorities reluctantly consented to remit the order for kneeling, they told him that he should not have his degree until he had publicly read in the Convocation House the following apology:—

'I. I do acknowledge all the crimes laid to my charge in the Black Book, and that I deserved the punishment imposed upon me.

' II I do acknowledge that the story of my being punished on account of my affection to King George and his illustrious house is unjust and injurious, not only to the reputation of the proctor, but of the whole university.

' III. I do profess sincerely that I do not believe that I was punished on that account.

' IV. I am very thankful for the clemency of the university in remitting the ignominious part of the punishment, viz. begging pardon on my knees.

' V. I beg pardon of Almighty God, of the proctor, and all the masters, for the offences which I have committed respectively against them; and I promise that I will, by my future behaviour, make the best amends I can for having offended by the worst of examples

Another contest ensued between Mr. Meadow-court and the authorities concerning the terms of this humiliating apology, which the offender, with proper spirit, refused to utter; whilst his adversaries maintained, with characteristic vindictiveness, that he should be stopped from his degree until he had spoken the penitential acknowledgment in the Convocation House. Eventually Mr. Meadowcourt gave his enemies a fall, and avoided the indignity which they sought to put upon him, by pleading in the Chancellor's Court the Act of Grace which the king had promulgated in behalf of a special class of political offenders. The plea was admitted, and thus the Whig partisan escaped further punishment by pleading that he was included in the declaration which condoned the offences of Jacobite plotters against the house of Hanover. A more comical conclusion to the squabble it is impossible to imagine; and the defeat of the Tory dons was not rendered less ridiculous by two subsequent denials in congregation of the offender's right to his degree.

After taking his degree, instead of sinking into political inactivity, Mr. Meadowcourt renewed his attacks upon the enemy, and brought the prevailing disloyalty of his university directly under the notice of the government, doubtless hoping thereby to secure for himself the patronage of the king's advisers.

'A most impudent and seditious sermon the author of ' Terræ-Filius' records, 'far exceeding everything that Mist or any such traitorous scribbler has published, was preached before the university on the twenty-ninth of May, 1719, by one W—n, a fellow of Merton College and the professor of poetry. Complaint was made of this sermon to the Vice-Chancellor by Mr. Meadowcourt, a fellow of Merton College; but the Vice-Chancellor refusing to proceed against the preacher upon this complaint, Mr. M. sent up an account of the sermon, and of the Vice-Chancellor's refusal to proceed against the preacher, to Mr. Secretary Craggs. After this account had been laid before the Lords Justices, their Excellencies ordered, that a letter should be wrote to Mr. M. to thank him for the commendable and becoming zeal that he had expressed for the honour of his Majesty, and to assure him of their favour and encouragement. After this, he was sent for by their Ex-cellencies to London, where he was long employed in the prosecution of this affair, which he managed so much to the satisfaction of their Excellencies that, it is said, he received the strongest promises of a considerable and speedy reward, Upon the strength of these promises he waited above half a year in London, and then returned to Oxford.

'After his return, the Constitutioners never met again together, either publickly or privately, as a club.

'Since the decease of this society, Whiggism itself in Oxford has almost expired. The Whigs, being now without leaders, and without a centre of unity, are shattered and broken into different parties and factions among themselves. Many have revolted to the Tory party, either out of fear of disgrace and oppression; or in hopes of academical honour and preferments. The rest, though they still retain their integrity, yet they are too well convinced that they ought to moderate and restrain their zeal for the best cause in the world, since the merit of suffering for it has been their only reward.'

Of course, such a publication as 'Terra Filius,' overflowing with virulence and personal animosities, must be read with caution and large allowance for the violence of the writer's prejudices. No one can urge that it is innocent of flippancy, and the usual faults of partisan literature. Other qualities of a still more reprehensible kind qualify its statements. But there is no lack of evidence in contemporaneous writings that the one-sided and occasionally scurrilous author of the scandalous papers gives a truthful picture of the poli-tical condition of the university in the days of Anne and the first George.

CHAPTER XV.

NICHOLAS AMHURST.

SOMETHING more in the way of consideration that the notice heretofore taken of him is due to Nicholas Amhurst, whose saucy and rather ribald pen enraged the dons, and made laughter for their enemies, whilst it perfected the ruin of the ready writer. Is it wrong in the author to cherish a pitiful sympathy for the academic 'black-sheep who, at Oxford, gave to drink and wild talk the hours which he should have devoted to studious labour, and, after his expulsion from Oxford, assailed, with impotent vindictiveness, the grave and reverend elders of the academy from which he had been ejected?

Certainly my sympathy is not with him because I regard him as a martyr to despotic and hypocritical pedagogues. It seems to me that he failed to make out his case against the doctors and proctors whom he denounced, and that, though they may have sinned against him in certain respects, they were fully justified in saying, 'Young man, you have considerable parts, but your residence in Oxford is productive of so much scandal and disorder, that you must oblige us by leaving the seat of learning; your undeniable cleverness and smartness are no reasons why we should endure your insolence, or permit you any longer to bring us into contempt with our pupils; you do us harm and yourself no good by dwelling amongst us; so, be off with you.' Dr. Delaune may have been indecorously fond of good wine, and he may now and then have played with dice for imprudently high stakes; but, whatever the doctor's errors and indiscretions, I have no doubt that he was, upon the whole, an honest gentleman, and that he obeyed a sense of duty, rather than a personal spite, when he ordered Mr. Nicholas Amhurst to pack up his traps and be gone from St. John's College. As much may also be said in behalf of the Vice-Chancellor, proctors, and other dignitaries, concerned in bringing about the young man's final scholastic humiliation. And yet, whilst recognizing the outrageous character of his misbehaviour, which compelled his superiors to put an indelible brand of disgrace upon him, I feel a certain friendship for the youngster, partly from the sympathy which every spectator of a conflict feels for the weaker combatant, if he fights pluckily; but chiefly because, in his wildest outbreaks of impudence and contumacy, the foolish fellow exhibited signs of honesty and generous spirit, which incline me to think that, had he been reproved more judiciously, and fallen under the correction of tutors naturally disposed to take large and charitable views of youthful delinquencies, he might have been reclaimed from evil ways, and made a useful member of society.

'It was under your wise instruction,' the young 'irreconcilable' wrote, in the flippant and bitter letter which he addressed to Dr. Delaune, after his ejection from St. John's, 'that I first arrived at any knowledge of the world; I came to your college a raw, ignorant schoolboy, and foolishly thought mankind in earnest in what they professed; I took liberty for a *real* blessing, and religion for the *real* worship of God; I often remember how scrupulous I was in the most common concerns of life; with what awful dread I took an oath, and with what tremendous veneration I received the sacrament; but how much I am improved by the *better* since, let my worst enemies bear witness.' Coming to the university with no lack of religious fervour and conscientiousness, the boy encountered persons and customs that animated him with a spirit of op position to the rulers of the place, whom he soon learnt to regard as prodigies .of hypocrisy and malevolence. He came into collision with dons more pompous than wise, with tutors indifferent to the intellectual and moral interests of their pupils, with divines whose lives were at direct variance with their professions; and he fell into the young reformer's common error, of charging upon an entire class the faults of a few conspicuous individuals. Having thus exaggerated the evils of the place and period, he made the still more fatal mistake of supposing that he could amend the abuses which he magnified, and correct the vices of society, by writing saucy lampoons against his official superiors. Associating himself with the violent Whigs, he made open war upon the respectabilities of the academic world,—a course that severed him from the decorous members of the university, and provoked the hostility of the Jacobite scholars, whilst it drew around him certain disorderly and dissolute students from whom he should have been most careful to hold himself aloof.

Called to account by the chiefs of his college, he made light of their expostulations, and in reply to their menace of extreme punishment, wrote the seriocomic verses entitled 'Advice to myself on being threatened to be expelled :'—

Prithee, dear Nick, thy wicked life amend,
And take the counsel of thy nearest friend;
No more, presumptuous boy, with impious airs,
Prefer the tempting bottle to thy prayers;
No more at Newnham, nor at Woodstock dine;

Abandon Finmore's Ale and Richmond's Wine;
No more by water, nor on horseback rove,
Nor mind the gadding girls in Maudlin Grove;
Cease with repeated crimes to urge the spleen
Of the grave Vice and silver-buttoned Dean;
Ah ! that with them alone thou hadst to strive,
For they are candid both, and will forgive;
But crowds of every species are thy foes,
Fops, ladies, critics, parsons, wits and beaux:
All these united with revengeful hate,
Vow thy destruction and conspire thy fate.
Crassus on thee contracts his wrathful brows,
And Semivir thy speedy ruin vows :
Whither expelled, for succour wilt thou run ?
Thy fortune squandered, and thy fame undone ?
A dark blind room in Grub Street wilt thou take,
And venal ditties for thy living make ?
Wilt thou in love-odes, or in satire deal,
Translate old authors, or from modern steal ?
In mournful elegiac rhimes complain,
Or try thy fate in the dramatic strain ?
These all are arts, in which but few prevail,
For one that gets a dinner, twenty fail.
Or wilt thou rather, studious of success,
Lay schemes with Curll, and ply the spurious press
By fraud and artifice obtain renown,
And with decoying titles cheat the town;
Whilst he shall grant thee, to reward thy flight,
At noon a dinner, and a glass at night ?
No, this to want and infamy will lead,
Soon will he turn thee off, when none will read;
Think thou betimes, thy former course forsake,
Espouse the church at last, and quit the rake;

Check thy free-thinking vein, thy sins acknowledge,
And grow a dull, old Fellow of a College.'

It would have been well for Nick Amhurst could he have conformed to such prudent advice. To be dull is better than to be disreputable. But there was a devil in his blood impelling him to ruin. Extending his hostility from the official teachers of religion to the religion which they taught, he became the ribald, derisive, impious creature that our pious ancestors used to designate ' Free-thinker' and Infidel,'— not a reverential free enquirer, but a flip-pant scoffer. New offences brought upon him the threatened punishment; and after his expulsion from Oxford he became a scribbler for booksellers, and made acquaintance with all the degrading experiences which, he had clearly foreseen, would ensue from his persistence in dissipation and unruliness.

For some few years after his expulsion he made a stir amongst the Grub Street writers, winning a transient notoriety in coffee-rooms by his satirical papers against the Oxonian Tories, and in return for services, which did them little good, whilst they consummated his social destruction, receiving the bootless patronage of a few third-rate chiefs of the Whig party. Between June 11, 1721, and July 6,. of the same year, he published the fifty numbers of the 'Terrse Filius,' a periodical in imitation of the ' Spectator in which he pelted his enemies ' the dons' with libellous accusation and malicious pleasantry. That much of this publication is scandalous and wearisome we have already intimated; but the Oxonian, who takes pleasure in realizing the social condition of his university in past time, may do worse things in the way of diversion than spend an hour over its pages.

In support of which qualified and carefully limited commendation of a scandalous series of sketches, I would refer the reader to the papers which describe the lighter humours of Queen Anne's Oxford, and set forth the unrefined amusements in vogue with the Oxonians of George the First's time.

In No. 31, addressing all gentlemen schoolboys, in his Majesty's dominions, who are designed for the university of Oxford,' the satirist says, ' For method's sake I shall address myself herein to such of you as belong to the public schools of London and Westminster; but my admonitions will be equally useful to all of you in general. I observe, in the first place, that you no sooner shake off the authority of the birch, but you affect to distinguish yourselves from your dirty school-fellows by a new suit of drugget, a pair of prim ruffles, a new bobwig, and a brazen-hilted sword; in which tawdry manner you strut about the town for a week or two before you go to college, giving yourselves airs at coffee-houses and booksellers' shops, and intruding yourselves into the company of us men; from all' which, I suppose you think yourselves your own masters, no more subject to controul or confinement Alas! fatal mistake ; soon will you confess that the tyranny of a school is nothing to the tyranny of a college; nor the grammar pedant to the academical one: for what signifies a smarting back to a bullied conscience ? What was Busby in comparison to Delaune ?

' After you have swaggered about town for some time, and taken your leave of all your old aunts and acquaintance, you set out in the stage-coach to Oxford, with recommendatory letters in your pockets to somebody or other in the college, where you are to be admitted, who introduces you, as soon as you get there, amongst a parcel of honest, merry fellows, who think themselves obliged in point of honour and common civility to make you drunk, and carry you, as they call it, a corpse to bed; the next night you are treated as civilly again, and perhaps for three or four nights afterwards. This glorious way of living being new to you, it confirms the notion you had conceived, upon throwing away your satchels, that you are no longer boys, but men, at your own disposal, and at liberty to follow your own inclinationa

' But let us now suppose this honey-week of jollity and drunkenness over : you are admitted into the college, and matriculated into the university; you have taken the oaths to observe the statutes of both; you have subscribed thirty-nine articles of religion, and paid your fees: in short, I will suppose you no longer strangers, but students, adopted babes of our venerable Alma Mater.'

By what means the 'adopted babes' changed themselves into Oxford ' Smarts,' as the idlest and most modish scholars of Nick Amhurst's university were pleased to term themselves, the reader may learn from the following paper, No. 46 of the ' Terrae Filius' series :—

' Having spoken pretty freely, in a former paper or two, of Oxford manners, I find that I have given great offence to a large body of fine gentlemen there who are called Smarts, one of whom reprimands me in the following letter lately received, which is valuable for several expressions:—

' " TO TERRÆ FILIUS.

' " *Christ Church College, July* 1.

' " MR. PRATE-APACE,—Amongst all the vile trash and ribaldry with which you have lately poisoned the public, nothing is more scandalous and saucy than your charging our university with the want of civility and good manners. Let me tell you, sir, for all your haste, we have as well-bred, accomplished gentlemen in Oxford, as anywhere in Christendom : men that dress as well, sing as well, dance as well, and behave in every respect as well, though I say it, as any men under the sun. You are the first audacious Wit-would that ever called Oxford a boorish, uncivilised place; and, demure sir, you ought to be horsed out of all good company for an impudent, praggish jackanapes. Oxford a boorish place! Poor wretch! I am sorry for thy ignorance. Who wears finer lace, or better linen, than Jack Flutter ? who has handsomer tie-wigs, or more fashionable cloaths, or cuts a bolder bosh, than Tom Paroquet ? Where can you find a handier man at a tea-table than Robin Tattle ? or, without vanity, I may say it, one that plays better at ombre than him, who subscribes himself an enemy to all such pimps as thou art,

' " VALENTINE FRIPPERY."

' That my readers may judge the better of Mr. Frippery's letter, I will give them a short description of the man himself He is a smart of the first rank, and is one of those who come, in their academical undress, every morning between ten and eleven to Lyne's coffee-house; after which he takes a turn or two upon the park, or under Merton-Wall, whilst the dull regulars are at dinner in their hall, according to statute; about one he dines alone in his chamber upon a boiled chicken, or some pettitoes; after which he allows himself an hour at least to dress in, to make his afternoon appearance at Lyne's; from whence he adjourns to Hamilton's about five; from whence (after strutting about the room for a while, and drinking a dram of citron) he goes to chapel, to show how genteelly he dresses, and how well he can chaunt. After prayers he drinks tea with some celebrated toast, and then waits upon her to Maudlin Grove, or Paradise Garden, and back again. He seldom eats any supper, and never reads anything but novels and romances.

' When he walks the streets, he is easily distin-guished by a stiff, silk gown, which rustles in the wind as he struts along; a flaxen tie-wig, or sometimes a long, natural one, which reaches down to his legs; a broad, bully-cocked hat, a square cap of above twice the usual size; white stockings, thin Spanish-leather shoes; his clothes lined with tawdry silk, and his shirt ruffled down the bosom as well as at the wrists. Besides all which marks, he has a delicate jaunt in his gait, and smells very philosophically of essence.

' This is the true description of my correspondent; and I leave the reader to judge whether this is properly good breeding, or ridiculous grimace, and inconsistent college foppery. There is not, I agree with Mr. Frippery, a deficiency of this sort of politeness in Oxford; but a man, in my opinion, may be very ill mannered under a silk gown, and do very uncivil things, for all he wears lawn ruffles. For instance, why may not one of these well-dressed sparks curse all strangers, or knock them down (provided he has a mob to defend him), as well as a ragged servitor of Jesus, or an half-starved scholar of St John's ? Is he ever the better bred for being better clad? Or do good manners consist in tufts or silk stockings? That a gay suit of clothes often hides a bad skin, and that a light wig sets off a dirty countenance, I am well enough convinced ; but that they can hide too a multitude of rudeness and ill manners, or atone for them, is what I never yet read either in Holy Scripture or profane philosophy. I should not, for my part, like a kick ever the better for having it from a red-topt shoe; nor do I think that a broken skin would smart the less, though it were to be done with a clouded cane.

' I know it is an hard thing to make any of my wary readers believe that beaux can be quarrelsome; but I can assure them, upon the word and honour of an English author, that five or six years ago some twenty or thirty Oxford smarts did actually frighten three or four poor-spirited foreigners, and kick a Presbyterian parson out of a coffeehouse.

' My dear friends, the smarts have another very scurvy trick. Would they be content to be foppish and ignorant themselves (which seems to be their sole study and ambition), I could freely forgive them; but they cannot forbear laughing at everybody that obeys the statutes, and differs from them; or (as my correspondent expresses it in the proper dialect of the place) that does not "cut a bold bosh as they do." They have singly, for the most part, very good assurances; but when they walk together in bodies (as they often do), how impregnable are their foreheads! They point at every one they meet, laugh very loud, and whisper as loud as they laugh, " Demme, Jack, there goes a prig ! Let us blow the puppy up !" Upon which they all stare him full in the face, turn him from the wall as he passes by, and set up an hoarse laugh, which puts the plain, raw novice out of countenance, and occasions great triumph amongst the tawdry desparadoes.

' There is, I confess, one thing in which the aforesaid gownsmen are very courtly and well bred : I mean in paying their debts; for you are not to suppose that they wear all this rich drapery at their own proper costs and charges; all the smarts in Oxford are not noblemen and gentlemen-commoners, but chiefly of a meaner rank, who cannot afford to be thus fine any longer than their mercers, tailors, shoe-makers, and periwig-makers, will " tick " with them, which now and then lasts three or four years; after which they brush off and return, like meteors, into the same obscurity from whence they arose.

' I have observed a great many of these transitory foplings, who came to the university with their fathers (rusty, old country farmers) in linsey-wolsey coats, greasy sun-burnt heads of hair, clouted shoes, yarn stockings, flapping hats, with silver hat-bands, and long muslin neckcloths, run with red at the bottom. A month or two afterwards I have met them with bob-wigs and new shoes, Oxford cut: a month or two more after this, they appeared in drugget cloaths and worsted stockings; then in tye-wigs and ruffles; and then in silk gowns; till by degrees they were metamorphosed into compleat smarts, and cursed the old country *putts*, their fathers, with twenty foppish airs and gesticulationa

'Two or three years afterwards, I have met the same persons in gowns and cassocks, walking with demure looks and an holy leer; so easy (as a learned divine said upon a quite different occasion) is the transition from dancing to preaching, and from the bowling-green to the pulpit!

'To conclude, Oxford daily increases in fine cloaths and fine buildings; never were bricklayers, carpenters, taylers, periwig-makers, better incouraged there; every day discovers a new fashion, or a new stone-wall And if you will still ask whether good manners and learning increase proportionably, I have a very good answer to give:— *Non omnia possumus omnes*.'

At the end of this vivid and suggestive description of the 'fast university-men of his day, Nicholas Amhurst, with superfluous honesty and simple candour, adds, 'N.B. In imitation of the learned Dr. Fiddes, author of the apology for the Duke of Buckingham's epitaph, in answer to a freethinker, Terrae Films' thinks fit to declare, that he wrote the letter from Valentine Frippery himself, in order to introduce his thoughts upon this subject the better.'

Though Nicholas Amhurst, in some of his papers, charges the gay Oxonians with paying their honourable addresses to women of a degree beneath the lowest grade of gentlewomen, and makes light of the famous Oxford 'toasts,' as the daughters of tradesmen, or college-servants, he elsewhere lets us see that the young ladies, with whom the 'Smarts' practised the pleasant arts of flirtation in Magdalen Grove, and St. John's Gardens, were neither so meanly born, nor so poorly educated, as his more violent expressions of contempt for their class would lead us to imagine.

'I do not,' he observes at the close of an essay against the academic girl of the period, 'charge all the " Oxford toasts" with the same ill fame, or the same ill designs ; nor would I knowingly charge any one of them with any one thing, of which she is guiltless, but an Oxford toast, in the common acceptation of that phrase, is such a creature as I am now going to describe. She is born of mean estate, being the daughter of some insolent mechanick, who fancies himself a gentleman; and resolves to keep up his family by marrying his girl to a parson, or a schoolmaster; to which end, he and his wife call her " pretty Miss," as soon as she knows what it means, and send her to the dancing-schools, to learn her to hold up her head, and turn out her toes; she is taught, from a child, not to play with any of the dirty boys and girls in the neighbourhood, but to mind her dancing, and have a great respect for " the gown." This founda-tion being laid, she goes on fast enough of herself, without any assistance, except a hoop and a gay suit of cloaths. Thus equipt, she frequents the balls and public walks in Oxford; where it is a great chance, if she does not, in time, meet with some raw coxcomb or other, who is her humble servant; waits upon her home ; calls upon her again the next day ; dangles after her from place to place; and is at last, with some art and management, drawn in to marry her. She has impudence,—therefore she has wit; she is proud,—and therefore she is well bred; she has fine cloaths,—and therefore she is genteel.'

Whilst they seized every occasion to air their gallantry before damsels who, though they were somewhat more refined than the barmaids and serving-girls of the public taverns, belonged to no exemplary class of womankind, the satirist accuses the 'Smarts' of boorish incivility to foreigners, and maintains that 'Oxford manners' had become a proverbial expression for boorishness of style and demeanour.

' I am afraid,' he remarks, that our country will never shake off the infamy, which it has long lain under, of being fierce and inhuman to strangers, in which the greatest point of good manners consists, and in which most nations excel us. We are naturally of a surly, ill-natured, morose temper; and as far as I can find, education, which improves other people, makes us worse; for this brutish temper of mind is nowhere in England so conspicuous as at our universities, which are filled with a crowd of churls and pedants who, being full of themselves, despise all the world besides, and kick and spurn at all strangers that encroach upon their territories, looking upon them as spies and informers.

'I was once at a coffee-house in Oxford when a foreigner came in, and seeing a grave doctor sitting by the fireside, approached and accosted him in an handsome manner in Latin, telling him that he was a stranger, that he could not speak English, and should be glad to hold some conversation with him concerning the university, which he came to see. The doctor, for answer, gave him every now and then an ugly look, as if be were afraid of his pocket, and coldly replied to all the gentleman said or asked, " etiam domine," or " non domine ;' " ay, sir," or " no, sir," without giving him any satisfaction in what he desired to be informed of; in the meanwhile all the company was whispering and grinning, and staring at him. " Who is that impudent fellow there ? " says one. " D him," says another; " by his assurance I believe he is an Hanoverian." At last he went away with astonishment in his face, surprised, no doubt, to find a place which he had heard so much renowned for learning, filled with such grey-headed novices and reverend Hottentots.

'But the most flagrant instance of their deportment to strangers happened about three or four years ago, when some German and French gentlemen, belonging to Baron Bothmar, came to see the university. They had not been there long before a popular scandal was invented and reported about town that these gentlemen had at such a time, and in such a place (for the best lyars are always particular), drunk damnation to the university in a bumper, and kill'd a poor drawer, by forcing him to drink King George's health upon his knees, against his conscience, which were two equally heinous crimes. This story was immediately known in every corner of the university, and they could not walk the streets without being publicly insulted, having continually, when they went out of doors, a mob of black-coats at their heels, crying, " Down with them! These are the rascals that drank perdition to the university!" which continued several days. At last, as they were going through All Souls College one afternoon, some jovial, blades, who were sitting there over a pipe and bottle, jumped out of the window, and pelting them out of the college with large stones, followed them to their lodgings, and staid before the house two or three hours together, crying out, " D all strangers! particularly Frenchmen and Ha- noverians and swearing that they would have their blood before they went away.

'The next day the gentlemen (hearing upon what account they were thus inhumanly treated, and being conscious that they did not deserve it) went to Dr. Dobson, President of Trinity College,. who was at that time pro-Vice-Chancellor, and acquainted him with the outrage committed upon them by the scholars, and upon what pretence ; at the same time they all took an oath that none of them, nor any in their company, did at any time drink perdition to the university, or any words to that effect, and therefore demanded satisfaction for the affronts they had received But they were told by that worthy magistrate that in all probability the gentlemen were in liquor (a very excusable thing in the university), or they would not have been guilty of such a piece of rudeness, and therefore it would be hard to punish them for it. Thus were they dismissed without any reparation, even that common one of having their pardon asked.

' If this was not a sufficient specimen of their brutality to strangers, I could produce out of their own historians various instances of an implacable spirit always prevailing amongst them against aliens of all sorts, even Jews, Papists, and the best of churchmen, but I forbear to do it, being sensible that many people will say that they ought to be commended, instead of ridicul'd, for what I shall allege and prove against them ; it being the great and distinguishing characteristicks of a true-born Church-of-England man to love none but his country and his own religion

That Nicholas Amhurst's sketches of Oxonian men and manners are satirical caricatures rather than veracious portraitures no reader will fail to discern who reflects that Addison, and gownsmen of Addisonian type, gave the tone to a considerable proportion of the scholars against whom ' Terrae-Filius,' in language of significant violence, prefers charges of boorish brutality, sottishness, profligacy, and contemptible frivolity. The critical reader, moreover, will not fail to bear in mind that Nicholas Amhurst belongs to the class of questionable, though not incompetent, witnesses whose testimony must always be received with caution and large allowances for the influences of passion and prejudice. But after perusing the ' Terras Filius' papers with the suspicion due to the testimony of a writer actuated by personal resentments, and a malicious desire to blacken the fame of the university from which he had been expelled with ignominy, the impartial student is constrained, by the evidence of contemporary literature, to admit that the essayist attacked real evils, and that his exaggerated statements were not altogether devoid of truth and honest purpose. The age of the Oxford Stuarts was also the age of the Mohocks, whose brutal tastes and enormities stirred the gentle Addison with unaccustomed indignation; and whilst it was the mode with fine gentlemen of the metropolis to vie with each other in debauchery and ruffianism, the roysterers and libertines of the colleges were not innocent of ruffianism, unknown amongst English gentlemen of these politer days.

CHAPTER XVI.

COMMEMORATIONS.

FROM an early period in the history of the university the scholastic exercises and festive usages of the Oxford Act aimed at the glorification of learning, rather than the commemoration of erudite and illustrious men, whose influence had been greatly beneficial to the guild of teachers. Year after year, though with occasional intermissions of the annual triumph, the speeches of successive vice-chancellors and proctors, the disputations of commencing graduates, and the oratorical buffooneries of the terræ-filii had celebrated scholarly pursuits, and incidentally magnified the achievements of famous students, beneath the roof of St. Mary's Church in times prior to the erection of the Sheldonian Theatre. The festival which celebrated the formal opening of the theatre was an affair of unusual magnificence and splendour ; but, though it comprised new diversions and was marked by departures from ancient usage, it should be regarded as the repetition of a long-established practice, rather than the institution of a new holiday. The scene was new, the entertainment presented several novelties, and the theatrical provisions and appliances far surpassed the arrange ments by which the graduates and students of old times imparted dramatic effect to their ceremonious performances in St. Mary's nave. But the origin and chief purposes of the demonstration were of venerable antiquity.

The proceedings of the first jubilation in the Sheldonian Theatre were repeated yearly, with no long interruptions, from the days of Charles the Second till the middle of the eighteenth century with Conservative adherence to the precedents created by that momentous rejoicing. Now and then circumstances may have compelled the omission of the annual festivals. More than once a terræ-filius *was kicked out of the theatre by the auditors whom his licentious abusiveness had offended; and after several intermissions of the* terræ-filial performances, the official jesters were finally suppressed as incurable and unendurable social nuisances. But the extinction of the caustic fools merely relieved the Act rejoicings of a diverting or irritating feature, without changing the general character of the entertainment. Again, no rule was observed in restraint of the number of classic compositions, in verse or prose, which the scholars recited to their auditors under Sheldon's roof. Allowance, however, being made for variations in these and other matters of detail, the theatrical rejoicings at an Oxford Act, in the earlier part of the eighteenth century, were almost perfect repetitions of the Act celebrations of Charles the Second's later years.

Readers who wish to see how the Act holiday was kept at Oxford in George the Second's reign may gratify their curiosity by perusing ' The Oxford Act, A.D. 1733. Being a Particular and Exact Account of that Solemnity. Wherein is inserted, for the Use of the Beau Monde, an Imitation of the First Part of the Bellus Homo et Academicus: or Part of the Dialogue between the Gay and the Plain Student. In a Letter to a Friend in Town. 1735.' From all that appears on the face of this tract I am inclined to think that the doctors, masters, noblemen, and ladies, who thronged the theatre on this occasion, must have been prodigiously bored by the twenty-seven Latin compositions which were recited by members of the university. If I gave my readers a specimen of the ' Bellus Homo et Academicus they would not thank me, though it may be presumed that each of the twenty-seven reciters was vociferously applauded by an assembly of hearers who were all the more disposed to seek diversion in noise because they had gained little by listening. The Oxonian correspondent, however, was well pleased with all he saw and heard at the musical performance, of which he remarks, ' The great Mr. Handel showed the way with his *Esther* — an oratorio or sacred drama—to a very numerous audience, at five shillings a ticket;' and at the subsequent *Theatri Encaenia*, which he defines as ' the celebration of the annual festival, *held in honour of the theatre*.'

Before the Act-rejoicing had come to be thus described as a jubilation in honour of the theatre, the aim and significance of the old celebrations had been generally lost sight of, and the time was fast approaching for the institution of the festival of Commemoration,— the annual demonstration that, regarded from one point of view, may be said to have grown out of the old Act, and, regarded from another ground of observation, may be said to have sprung from a distinct source before it superseded the Act holiday of olden time. There are antiquaries who maintain warmly that Commemoration is nothing else than the old Act festival under a new name and dress. On the other hand, there are those who —taking, as it appears to me, a more correct view of the subject—recognize in Commemoration nothing more than a modern revival of the ecclesiastical wake, which circumstances induced the university to substitute for the yearly triumph that had its origin in remote usage.

But however widely Oxonians may differ respecting the history of Commemoration, they agree in thinking it the greatest festival of the university calendar, and in maintaining that, though it may be something less than a national, it is much more than a mere local, holiday.

All the social arrangements of the Oxford summer terms point to Commemoration. It is the concluding triumph of the academic year, anticipated by the world without, scarcely less than by the world within the proctor's jurisdiction. Dons and undergraduates look forward to it with equal interest. Weeks before the days especially appropriated to it, the university begins to put on her holiday attire and to exhibit signs of pleasure-making. Country clergymen come up to engage lodgings for their wives and daughters, and find all the best apartments taken by undergraduates for their mothers and sisters. Soon the ladies appear upon the scene; some with sons at Boniface or St. Dunstan's, thinking how few and short the years appear since (a quarter of a century back) they witnessed a commemoration for the first time in their lives, and for the first time let love into their simple hearts; others, high-bred English girls, well pleased with themselves and all this worlds arrangements, save and except that they *do* think it rather hard that girls cannot be undergraduates.

Daily, more of these gentle visitors appear, gliding under the dark walls of University College, and through the quiet cloisters of Magdalen,—their slender forms, and impalpable bonnets, and silks of every delicate hue, giving a new charm to the vistas and lawns of college gardens. It is pleasant to hear their voices in sombre libraries and corridors. Their light steps on the Bodleian floors are an unwont music. The spirit with which they throw themselves into the life of the place is scarcely less refreshing to behold than the amount of work and pleasure they get through in a, fortnight or three weeks is wonderful to witness. In a trice they are familiar with every detail of university millinery; can distinguish at a glance between the robes of masters, bachelors, commoners, scholars, and noblemen ; and, for a box of kid gloves, would cut you out a doctor's scarlet gown. In four-and-twenty hours they have become adepts in all the gossip, and rivalries, and scandal—ay, even the slang—of Alma Mater. One never finds them tripping as "to the speciality of a particular college—the aristocratic éclat of Christ Church, the mild respectability of Pembroke, the rural tranquillity of Worcester, the boating and scholarship of Balliol.

In homage to these ' lionesses the arts of the toilet rise in university estimation. The venerable master of St. Antony's orders out his new gaiters. The Vicegerent of Hertford—who, notwithstanding his erudition and irreproachable Latin prose, is, it must be confessed, *rather* too careless of appear-ances—brushes the snuff from the lappels of his capacious waistcoat, and consents to wear gloves. As for the more youthful of Alma Mater's *alumni* , the record of their personal splendour is to be found in certain books, kept according to the everlasting laws of double entry. But a little extravagance and personal vanity are pardonable in young men whose sweet labour it is to attend ' lionesses' to Blenheim and Cumnor, to boat-races and choral services, to 'punt them under the leafy shade of the Cherwell, to make up water-parties to Newn-ham.

With a bewildering succession of breakfasts, lunches, dinners, suppers, horticultural shows, *fStes* , aquatic sports, masonic balls, concerts, sermons, and processions, the carnival of the scholars approaches its brilliant consummation. On Sunday is the throng in the Broad Walk, On Wednesday, come the pomp and the speeches, the uproar and the crush of the theatre. Possibly, in the breaks between the innumerable banquets of the next Commemoration, some readers of these Memorials may like to retire from the stir and tumult, and, away from the bray of martial music and the peal of deeply-rolling organs, in some quiet nook of Addison's Walk or Christ-Church Meadows, con the following notes on scholastic holidays of past times.

Social customs are bonds uniting distant gen-erations and establishing kinship between different families of our race. The Eleusinia and the Harvest Home, the Olympia and the Village Fair, the Feriae Autumnales and the Long Vacation, join hands over intervals of centuries; and in the mirth of our English Christmas is caught a faint echo from the riot of the Saturnalia, when the slave for a few brief days enjoyed security from the *hor-ribile flagellum,* made glad his heart with wine, and, decked in the garb of the freeman, bandied jests with his master. The festivals and sacred observances of ancient Athens and Rome still remain after the lapse of ages, altered in form, but similar in spirit; and through them the poetry of the present has received much of its loveliness and dignity from the religion of the past. Embracing all human sympathies, and giving expression to universal truths, they possessed a vitality that defied decay. Their doctrine was the teaching of the Preacher:—'To every thing there is a season, and a time to every purpose under the heaven: a time to weep, and a time to laugh; a time to mourn, and a time to dance

Prominent amongst the *dies feriati* of the early Christians were the days set apart to commemorate the dedication of their churches. Wisely imitating all that was good and pure of heathen and Jewish institutions, the framers of the Christian polity opened their temples with imposing ceremonies, in many respects closely resembling those which roused the religious enthusiasm of the multitudes gathered together at Jerusalem, ' at that time when ' Solomon held a feast, and all Israel with him, a great congregation with him, from the entering in of Hamath unto the river of Egypt, before the Lord our God, seven days and seven days, even fourteen days' When the lenient sway of Constantino restored the churches which the persecutions, of Diocletian had levelled with the ground, the Encaenia, or Feasts of Dedication, were solemnized in every region where Christianity had adherents. At these sacred festivities the bishops of neighbouring provinces assembled, and each in turn made an oration suitable to the occasion.

Revolutionary as to thought but conservative as to form, Christianity, instead of abolishing the pagan holidays, contented herself with reforming them. Those that were utterly impure, she suppressed; but the others she wisely retained, after purging them of old abuses and infusing them with a new spirit. In our own island, the temples which had been reared to false gods were renewed, and set apart to the one true religion ; and the very days, which had previously been devoted to the worship of devils, were proclaimed holidays to the glory of the Heavenly Father.

In obedience to Gregory's instructions, the En-caenia (of which Spelman observes, 'Haec eadem sunt quae apud Ethnicos paganalia dicebantur') were established in Great Britain. In every parish the consecration of the church was celebrated with an annual feast, usually kept on the day of the saint to whom the church was dedicated. At this sacred demonstration public thanks and praise were rendered, not only to the author of Christianity, but to those men, living or dead, who had contributed conspicuously to the erection or prosperity of the church. On the eves of these festivals prayers were offered up and songs sung all night through. Long after these vigils had been disused they continued to give the name of *wakes* to the holidays themselves. These wakes were amongst the most hearty and delightful features of the life of merrie England. The ordinary place of entertainment, in fine weather, was the churchyard, in which booths were erected, and all the whimsical jollifications of a country fair were encouraged. When the weather was foul, or any circumstances rendered it advisable to hold the holiday under cover, the riotous merry-making went on beneath the roof of the church. Feasting and music, mugs of foaming ale, mummers and morris-dancers, dames arrayed in gorgeous shawls, and girls tricked out with ribbons, miracle-plays and puppet-shows, wrestling and cudgel-playing, were the ornaments and amusements of the day. The gladness and humour of the scene are celebrated in Herrick's Hesperides':—

' Come, Anthea, let us two

Go to feast, as others do.
Tarts and custards, creams and cakes,
Are the junkets still at wakes;
Unto which the tribes resort,
Where the business is the sport.
Morris-dancers thou shalt see,
Marien, too, in pagentrie;
And a mimic to devise
Many grinning properties.
Players there will be, and those
Base in action as in clothes;
Yet with strutting they will please
The incurious villages.
Near the dying of the day
There will be a cudgel play.
When a coxcomb will be broke,
Ere a good word can be spoke.
But the anger ends all here,
Drencht in ale, or drown'd in beere.

Happy rustics best content
With the cheapest merriment,
And possess no other feare
Than to want the wake next yeare.'

The Puritans endeavoured to put an end to wakes. Stubbes, in his ' Anatomie of Abuses' (1585), inveighed against them as scenes of debauchery — impoverishing the poor and doing no good to the rich. 'The poore men he says, 'that beare the charges of these feastes and wakesses, are the poorer, and keep the worser houses a long time after. And no marvaile, for many spend more at one of these wakesses than in all the whole yere besides.' Doubtless Stubbes had truth and common sense on his side. Such was the extravagant hilarity of the holiday, that Spelman (although he distinguished between ' wakes — celebritates bacchanales' and 'holy wakes') was misled by it so far as to derive the term 'wake' from the Saxon word *wak*, signifying 'drunkenness.' In the same way Speght speaks of a wake as 'a drinking fit.' But against common sense were arrayed poetry, ancient usage, and the authority of the law. The *Book of Sports* says : ' His Majesty finds that, under pretence of taking away abuses, there hath been a general forbidding, not only of ordinary meetings, but of the feasts of the dedications of churches, commonly called wakes. Now his Majesty's express will and pleasure is, that these feasts, with others, shall be observed; and that his justices of the peace, in their several divisions, shall look to it, both that all disorders there may be prevented and punished, and that all neighbourhood and freedom, with manlike and lawful exercises, may be used.' Discouraged and in some places altogether suppressed by the Puritans of the Commonwealth, the wakes revived under the Restoration. The description of the wake in the *Spectator* (No. 161) differs little from Herrick's sketch. But towards the middle of the eighteenth century the wakes began to fall from popularity to comparative disregard, whence they in due course dropped into contempt Their religious purpose utterly lost sight of, they dwindled into village fairs and hoppings.'

Just when public feeling gave its final judgment against the commemorations of the pious founders of parish churches, a wake, on an almost unprecedented scale of splendour, was established at Oxford in honour of the benefactors of that university, but more especially in celebration of Nathaniel Lord Crewe, Bishop of Durham, whose name appears in the list of the benefactors of the university next to that of Dr. Eadcliffe, the unlettered physician whose donation to Oxford of the superb Radcliffe Library caused Garth to observe that ' it was as if an eunuch had founded a seraglio

At this date the orators of the Sheldonian Theatre and University Pulpit are about the only people to say much in favour of this prelate. Affecting the munificence and exceeding the pride of Wolsey, vain and false, a cringing time-server, unprincipled and ostentatious, but at the same time an accomplished courtier, plausible and ingratiating, Lord Crewe was, as a man and a priest, an ornament to his own age, though he would have been a scandal in the present. Descended from a line of lawyers, he possessed the subtlety of them all, but wanted their probity and moral courage. His great-grandfather was Sir Randolph Crewe, Knight, the Chief Justice of the Court of King's Bench, who was deprived of his office, November the 9th, 1626, because he disapproved of Charles the First raising money by loan. His grandfather was Sir Thomas Crewe, Serjeant-at-Law, and Speaker of the House of Commons in the last Parliament of James the First, and in the first of Charles the First The Serjeant's reputation as a lawyer was proverbial:—

' Would you have your cause go true,
Take senior Crooke and junior Crewe.'

And Charles the First only indorsed the popular opinion when he said, 'Thomas Crewe is against me, and yet he is an honest man.' The eldest son of the honest Sir Thomas, though bred to the law, never practised his profession. On the Restoration he was created a baron of the realm, by the title of Lord Crewe of Stene, in consideration of his services to the royal cause.

The fifth son of John Lord Crewe, Nathaniel, was born January 31st, 1633, and reared to the church. Even before his birth there were omens of his future greatness. His mother 'dreamed of a fine concert of music in the Rookery;' and to this dream was attributed the bishop's fondness for music. His education completed, his advancement in his profession was rapid. He was not forty years of age when he was made Bishop of Oxford, and he was only forty-one when he was permitted to purchase the rich bishopric of Durham from Nell Gwynne for about 6000*l*. But though he had risen through the Stuarts, and had been the mere crea-ture of their will, he did not deem it incumbent on him to fall with them. At the change of dynasty, however, his position was a perilous one. The compliant prelate, who had acted as the grand inquisitor of James the Second's Ecclesiastical Commission, and sanctioned its worst excesses, was menaced with punishment Although he had made mean overtures of reconciliation to the triumphant party, and was amongst those who voted in convocation (Feb. 6th, 1688-9) that James had abdicated the throne, he was excepted by name from the pardon of the 23rd May, 1690. Panic-struck, the prelate fled to Holland, and offered to resign his bishopric to Burnet, on condition that he received 1000*l*. per annum from its revenues. Affairs, however, took a favourable turn. He anointed Johnson's scourged back with a present of money, and he bribed his enemies to be silent. Returning to England, he lived, a Vicar of Bray amongst the bishops, into his eighty-ninth year, dying September 18, 1722, after being a bishop for fifty years, three months, and two days—for forty-seven years of which time he had occupied the see of Durham.

As he left no issue, the barony of Stene (to which he succeeded in 1691 through the death of his elder brothers) became extinct. The greater part of his wealth was bequeathed to Lincoln College (of which he had formerly been Rector), but he also left noble legacies to the university and to other colleges. Amongst these bequests was a sum of money to New College, the interest of which was to be expended in an annual festival. For a quarter of a century the members of New College enjoyed the exclusive benefits of the donation; but about the year 1750 the fellows transferred it to the university, to defray the expenses of a musical and miscellaneous entertainment in honour of its patrons and benefactors In accordance with universal custom, the different colleges had, of course, from their first establishment, held celebrations of their origin, founders, and benefactors. The annual 'feast days' and 'gaudy (or rejoicing) days' which are still maintained in the separate corporations of our universities, were at the commencement nothing more or less than college ' wakes;' the offices, still observed in the chapels on certain days in commemoration of founders, being in form and feeling similar to the panegyric thanksgivings which Christians offered up in grateful recollection of the founders of their churches.

In a spirit identical with that of the Commemoration offices, the names of the public benefactors of the university are introduced into the bidding prayer by the select preachers of the university pulpit. By the new entertainment (1750) it was proposed to accomplish on a more liberal and imposing scale, in honour of university benefactors, that which had from all antiquity been performed by colleges in memory of the munificent individuals who had created or contributed to their prosperity. Such was the origin of the annual festivities, at one time known as the Oxford Encaenia, or Lord Crewe's Encaenia, or Lord Crewe's Commemoration,—but now invariably mentioned as the Oxford Commemoration.

Since the institution of Commemorations, Oxford has had eight installations of Chancellors, the roll being composed of John Fane, Earl of Westmoreland; George Henry Lee, Earl of Lichfield; Frederick North, Lord North, afterwards Earl of Guildford; William Henry Cavendish Bentinck, Duke of Portland; William Wyndham Grenville, Lord Grenville; Arthur Wellesley, Duke of Wellington ; George Geoffrey Smith Stanley, Earl of Derby; and the present Marquis of Salisbury, whose scholastic erudition and brilliant parts qualify him in a high degree to be the official chief of the university.

The installation of the Earl of Westmoreland (1759) was immediately followed by Encaenia, which have ever since served as precedents for succeeding entertainments, as to their more important particulars. Previous to the Chancellor's arrival, the Vice-Chancellor and delegates issued five orders to the members of the university, of which No. 1 and No. 4 are interesting — the former illustrating the turbulence of the yoimger gownsmen a century since, and the latter apportioning the seats of the theatre in much the same manner as they are allotted at present:—

' 1. That the students appear nowhere abroad during the Chancellor's abode in the university without their caps and gowns suitable to their degree and condition, and that their apparel be such as the statutes require, and *that they behave with such order and decency as become gentlemen of a liberal education.*

' 4. That during his lordship's installation, and the following commemoration and encaenia, all persons repair to and keep their proper seats and places in the theatre. The rising semicircle of the theatre is reserved for the noblemen and doctors. The in-closure within the rail is the place for the Masters of Arts. The gallery behind the Doctors in the circular part of the theatre, and the east and westward side-galleries, are reserved for ladies and strangers, among whom all gownsmen are forbid to intermix. The upper gallery above the noblemen and doctors is appointed for Gentlemen-commoners and Bachelors ; and the upper-galleries, eastward and westward, are for undergraduate scholars of houses and Commoners. The rest of the area for batlers, servitors, &c'

The ceremony of Installation took place on Tues-day, July 2. ' Lord Crewe's Commemoration we are informed by the reporters of the period, began on Wednesday, the 4th, and lasted four days. On Wednesday ' the Commemoration Speech was spoken by Mr. Warton, the poetry professor in the theatre; after which the honorary degree of D.C.L. was conferred on certain noblemen and gentlemen, and * the Encaenia were continued by the following gentlemen ; viz., Hon. Mr. Beauclerk, of Queen's, English; Sir B. B. Delves, Magdalen College, Latin; Mr. Beckford, New College, English; Mr. Wodehouse and Mr. Le Maistre, Christ Church, Latin Dialogue; Mr. Nibbes, St. John's, Latin. All these exercises were performed with great propriety of elocution and action, and were highly applauded by the audience. In the evening was performed the oratorio of "Esther."'

The Encaenia were celebrated on the two following days in a similar manner; the audience, gathered together in the Sheldonian Theatre, being entertained with seven 'Encaenia or gratulatory exercises' on Thursday, and six on Friday, — on which last-mentioned day there was also performed, by the whole opera band,' in the same place, ' an Italian Ode, in praise of the Chancellor.' The festivities were closed on the following day by Dr. King with a spirited and eloquent oration.

The Instalment of the Earl of Lichfield (July, 1763) was in like manner followed by Commemoration. On the first day, after the Duke of Manchester, the Earl of Cork, and Mr. Trevor Hampden, had been made Doctors of Civil Law, the Duke of Beaufort, the Earl of Anglesey, and Lord Robert Spencer, and a fourth speaker (who, poor fellow, was so nervous that he could not articulate audibly) recited verses in honour of the peace, when a humorous, though scarcely novel, diversion was achieved by two students holding a Latin dialogue, the one of them representing an alderman of London, and the other an advocate for the peace. ' The characters were extremely well sustained, and the non-sensical objections of the discontented alderman were refuted with great spirit by his opponent, who spoke with much humour and emphasis, so as to draw frequent bursts of applause from the audienca Between these speeches there were intervals of music from the orchestra; and at one o'clock the assembly broke up *for dinner* . At three P.M., however, dinner over and wine pushed aside, the ladies and gentlemen returned to hear the 'Acis and Galatea.'

'Eight hours,' wrote one of the festive audience, 'in the theatre in one day, I rather the't unconscionable, and I don't doubt but many rosy feces I saw there were of the same opinion, and would have wished for less music and more wine. To many of the ladies, likewise, I fancy it would have been as agreeable not to have assembled so early in the morning, and to have spent the evening in private amusements.'

The Installation and Encaenia of 1773, when Lord North made his first appearance in Oxford as Chancellor, were on a scale of unprecedented magni-ficence. There were present so many ladies that they positively exceeded the men in number, not less than they surpassed them in costliness of costume.

But it was not till the festival following the Duke of Portland's public instalment (1793) that Oxford knew what a thorough crush meant The Duke brought with him a strong bevy of the highest noblesse. At the installation, the Duke of Devonshire and twelve other noblemen were honoured with the D.C.L. degree. Wyndham and Burke and Burke's ill-starred son were present. Copteston (afterwards Bishop of Llandaff) recited his Latin poem, ' Marius sitting among the ruins of Carthage and recitations of more than a score other essays in prose or verse were made during the Wednesday, Thursday, and Friday of the week. The ladies came in even greater force than they had done in 1773. They were dressed, with only a very few exceptions, in white, with ribbons of different colours ; and the undergraduates, from their eminence, instead of cheering ' the ladies in pink or ' the ladies in blue,' cheered 'the ladies with pink ribbons,' and ' the ladies with blue ribbons.' Three thousand persons forced their way into the Theatre, and hundreds turned away from the doors, unable to effect an entrance. The ladies were admitted first; and, until they were accommodated with seats, the gownsmen were kept outside. For a few minutes the expectant crowd in Broad Street maintained some approach to decorum, but soon they manifested signs of impatience. A score of the more athletic undergraduates climbed the rails. Then a rush was made at the gates, and they were forced. The uproar and confusion that followed were terrible. Gowns were torn to ribbons, caps were broken, men trodden under foot, and pugilistic rounds fought in every direction: in one case, the combatants being a Doctor of Divinity and a Master of Arts. ' The Broad' was literally strewed with shoes, buckles, gowns, hats, caps, and prostrate men. Numbers of pickpockets, who had come down from town, and assumed the M.A. costume, made a rich harvest of plunder from the crowd within the Theatre and the crowd that surged through the Schools, quadrangle. Mrs. Billington acted the part of vocal enchantress at Oxford in 1793, as Catalani did at Lord Gren-ville's installation in 1810, and as Jenny Lind did on a recent occasion ; and there was need for her dulcet strains to soothe the angry passions roused by that memorable fray.

On the occasion of Lord Derby's instalment, it was remarked that the enthusiastic reception awarded to Mr. Disraeli made the ovation his, and not the Earl's. A similar criticism might have been made on the acclamations with which Burke was honoured by the Oxonians of '93. His son, so soon to be taken before him to ' the silent world was made a D.C.L.; but the statesman, it is said, declined to enrol his own name 'amongst the doctors in consequence of what had previously occurred between himself and the university. But, wherever he went, he was hailed with a tempest of applause. The homage was rendered to the author of 'Reflections on the French Revolution rather than to the economical Reformer and the Whig Statesman who had written the ' Thoughts on the Cause of the Present Discontents.' Apart, however, from this cause of popularity, Burke's career had been of a kind eminently calculated to rouse the sympathies and elicit the admiration of generous and highly-educated young men cherishing sweet dreams of ambition, and trusting to arrive at power and eminence by their energy and mental endowments. ' Oxford men' have a hearty, genuine sympathy for any one who, by individual force of character, makes a great game against heavy odds

The Commemoration of 1810, presided over by Lord Grenville, very closely resembled that of 1793. Another fierce scramble and contest ensued in Broad Street, in which the ladies fared worse than on the prior occasion. ' At nine o'clock/ says an eye-witness, the outer gates of the theatre were opened, when ladies and gentlemen had their clothes actually torn to rags, and lost their shoes, rings, Ac. A number of rings and trinkets were afterwards picked up out of the mud.' The grave had long since closed over Burke, but another hero was in the theatre, conspicuous by his uniform, and surrounded with a halo of glory not yet dimmed. ' Three cheers more for Sir Sidney Smith.'

The tendency of all the alterations made of late years by the university authorities in the ceremonial of Commemoration has been in a right direction, as they have resulted in a great curtailment of the forms, and an equal expansion of the jovial element of the celebration. The public are no longer expected to spend the best part of each of the bright summer days in the stifling atmosphere and riot of the theatre. Nor are they any longer subjected to the infliction of a long succession of miserable recitations. The only scholastic compositions publicly delivered by the junior members of the university at the present time are those which have gained the Chancellor's prizes—the Latin Verse, Latin Prose, and English Prose, and the Newdigate Prize Poem in English verse. In some quarters it is the foolish fashion to speak of these productions superciliously, as youthful effusions that must be charitably overlooked How little they merit such detraction it is not my in-tention to show; but it is worth while to observe that the Prizemen of Oxford are intellectually the flower of the university—' the very best men of their time A survey of the Class Lists brings before one's notice crowds of highly-placed obscurities— scholars whose reputation for scholarship or power of any kind depends totally on the Class List in which their names appear. But the catalogues of Prizemen flash with the titles of the famous or the eminently successful. The first Chancellor's Prize for an English Prose Essay was awarded in 1768. Taking from the year 1769 to 1822 inclusive, we find nine out of the fifty-four English Essayists (i. e. one in six) fought their way into the ranks of the peerage, namely, J. Scott, Earl of Eldon; Henry Addington, Lord Sidmouth; T. Burgess, Bishop of Salisbury; C. Abbott, Lord Tenterden; H. Phillpotts, Bishop of Exeter; E. Copleston, Bishop of Llandaff; R Mant, Bishop of Down and Connor; R. Whately, Archbishop of Dublin; W. A. Shirley, Bishop of Sodor and Man. Nor are the remaining of the fifty-four names otherwise than distinguished. Some of them are familiar as household words ; such as Daniel Wilson, Bishop of Calcutta; Reginald Heber, Bishop of Calcutta; Sir John Taylor Coleridge; and Dean Milman. Of the Prizemen since the year 1822 we do not speak, for obvious reasons : the majority of them being still young men, with a wide extent of the battle-field of life still before them; and some being in the critical period that divides brilliant social distinction from mere substantial prosperity. In some cases the victors have gained double honours. Thus, Sir John Taylor Coleridge and Dean Milman were Latin Essayists as well as English. It is worthy of remark, also, that the Latin Verse Prize seems to have more charms for patrician scholars than either of the other two. Amongst the winners of that palm are W. W. Grenville, Lord Grenville (1779); R. Wel-lesley, Marquis of Wellesley (1780); the Earl of Derby (1819); the Earl of Carlisle (1821), who also, in the same year, gained the Newdigate.

If the speeches as they are at present managed are an appropriate *finale* to the Academic holiday, the other features of the Sheldonian ceremony are not less commendable. What Oxford man has not a pleasant recollection of the heat, the crush, the frantic uproar of the theatre? If the authorities wished to suppress it, they could easily put an end to the riot. If ' the lionesses instead of being ranged apart by themselves, were assigned seats in every part of 'the house the undergraduates' gallery would be not a whit less decorous and ' proper' than the Doctors' semicircle. But then the ladies would no longer have the enjoyment of hearing ' those young men make such a terrible noise That noise, moreover, has its uses. It subdues the insolence of office, and is in every respect an admirable form for public opinion to express itself in. Many a bilious proctor has been prevented from exceeding the proper limits of his duty by a wholesome dread of being hissed and hooted at Commemoration in the presence of the ladies. Moreover, the row is jolly. Three days of incessant champagne and epigrams have their effect on the strongest nerves. There is a point in a sustained outburst of hilarity when the staunchest and boldest find themselves oscillating between a rapturous joy and a sense of impending calamity. At such a crisis it is an agreeable relief to escape from the conflict of feeling, and, with a noble disregard of all considerations of dignity or interest, throw oneself into universal uproar.

CHAPTER XVII.

OXFORD IN THE FUTURE.

IN an early part of this survey of the rise and progress of the university we detected the germ of the modern collegiate system in the victory of the inmates' over the ' chums and the consequent orders that all students should be entered on the roll and subject to the discipline of some one of the numerous boarding-schools. We next witnessed the rivalry between the endowed and the unendowed houses, and saw how the former, after pushing the latter out of business and existence, monopolized the privileges and powers of the university, — a monopoly which Laud's Caroline Code recognized and confirmed in a manner that contributed greatly to its endurance.

Of the collegiate system which thus came into existence in mediaeval time, and gradually acquired the absolute control of the academic community, it may be remarked that, whatever the advantages accruing from its operation, it weakened and almost extinguished the affection which the students of old time cherished for the entire scholastic community. It broke the whole into parts, and substituted the sentiment of collegiate attachment for the sentiment of devotion to Alma Mater. In conversation 'college' gradually usurped much of the signification that had in ancient time belonged to 'university The title of' collegian' pushed that of university student' out of fashion. Instead of being described as a man who had been educated ' at the university the Oxonian graduate was more generally said to have * been at college;' and though Alma Mater has recently been liberated, to a certain extent, from the tyranny of the collegiate system, years and generations must pass ere the university will recover from her subjection to the colleges. For many a day the Christ-Church man will continue to be prouder of belonging to Christ Church than of being a member of the university.

Expatiating on the merits and beauties of the collegiate system — of which, by the way, his personal knowledge was very slight — Dr. Johnson remarked: ' There is here, sir, such a progressive emulation. The students are anxious to appear well to their tutors; the tutors are anxious to have their pupils appear well in college ; the colleges are anxious to have their students appear well in the university; and there are excellent rules of discipline in every college. That the rules axe sometimes ill observed may be true, but is nothing against the system. The members of an university may, for a season, be unmindful of their duty. I am arguing for the excellency of the institution That circumstances may have disposed the man of letters to take too favourable a view of institutions, which he observed during the least honourable period of their comparatively recent history, I do not deny. A little pressure would perhaps induce me to admit that he is chargeable with glossing abuses, which required exposure, and for which no sufficient apology could be framed. But, confining their regard to the requirements of the past, few of my readers will decline to coincide with the doctor's commendation of the theory and general practice of the system.

So far as this work is concerned, I have no intention to figure as an acrimonious witness against the present condition of the colleges or their policy in former time. Having hitherto mixed this cup of new thought and old story with a view to rendering it palatable to Oxonians of all ages and degrees, though especially agreeable to gownsmen of the younger and lighter sort, I do not purpose at this late stage of the brewing to give it a flavour which would occasion dissatisfaction or disgust to any of the readers whom I am chiefly desirous to gratify. Not, be it observed, that I am vain and simple enough to hope that my efforts to illustrate the story of a splendid seat of learning may elicit acclamations of approval in senior common-rooms. Enthusiasm is neither the virtue nor the frailty of dons.' All that I presume to desire from them is, the frigid and carefully limited approbation, the merciful forbearance from censure, the stately manifestation of supercilious amusement, by which beings of superior intelligence and lordly style condescend, in their most benevolent moments, to recognize the meritorious services and dutiful in-tentions of ordinary mortals. And that I may not miss the highest reward to which a frail and altogether human writer can reasonably aspire, I will say nothing to provoke the terrible anger of a body of august and infinitely learned personages, whom I regard with the profoundest reverence.

Not mine, therefore, the pen to prefer angry charges of incapacity and sloth against collegiate teachers—not mine the task to demonstrate that the system, which has flourished in our universities during these later centuries, is chiefly remarkable for the protection it extends, and for the prosperity it affords, to negligent, if not incompetent, lecturers, who, after extracting from undergraduates high fees for inefficient instruction, leave them to buy of 'private coaches' the assistance which the abundantly remunerated tutors of the various colleges are presumed, by the theory of the college-system, to render to the members of their classes. To some less complaisant and just scribe the reader must have recourse, who wishes to be assured that the collegiate system not long since teemed with the characteristic and most pernicious evils of protective organizations; that whilst denying to the poor student, for whose welfare it professed to provide, the right to purchase tutorial counsel in open market of the most liberal dealers, it too often constrained him to spend his slender store of cash on miserable counterfeits of the commodities of which he stood in need; and that, even when it furnished him with a little sound instruction at an exorbitant price, it made his interest an altogether secondary consideration to the interest of the corporation which stood between him and his Alma Mater. Of such invective I am no distributor. Mine is a loving-cup for which such gall is no fit ingredient.

Nor, if I were less desirous to compound a grateful beverage, or altogether indifferent as to the effect of my cup, could I honestly speak much ill of the collegiate system as it came under my observation some twenty years since, or of the tutors who then ministered to the intellectual wants of Oxford undergraduates. I do not say that the university had no pupils who gave little heed to studious concerns, or that it had no teachers of inferior parts and insufficient earnestness. Of course I could tell of nominal students who were allowed to run a short course of boyish profligacy and idleness to a state of degradation, from which no proper care was taken to preserve them. On the other hand, I could give some equally racy and painful stories of tutors who had no moral fitness for their vocation, and who regarded their classes of pupils merely as so many companies of tiresome youngsters about whom they knew little, and wished to know less. But it would be a gross libel on the Oxford of my recollection if I were to maintain that such 'dons' and undergraduates were fair representatives of the intellectual and moral condition of the university.

It would, I am of opinion, be impossible to name a period when the collegiate system was more efficiently carried out than it was during my term of pupilage. And whilst I venture to give this deliberate testimony respecting the general state of the university, I may remark that the college, in which my days were chiefly spent, was fortunate, in having rulers who exerted themselves strenuously and successfully to make it a model of academic discipline. Its tutors were men of great natural abilities and large attainments; and whilst all of them displayed abundant zeal and conscientiousness in the performance of their duties, one of them habitually exceeded the obligation of his office in discharging the teacher's functions, and never appeared more cordially delighted than when he discerned in a freshman the ability and disposition to derive the greatest possible measure of advantage from good training. And the general government of the house was no less exemplary than the action of its tutorial staff

To raise his comparatively small and slightly endowed house to pre-eminence over greater and wealthier colleges was beyond Francis Jeune's power, but he effected wonders for the society of which he was for several years the chief ruler. He gave it honourable status in the Class-lists, procured the enlargement of its buildings, reformed its economy for the benefit of students of narrow means, and was no less judicious than indefatigable in his endeavours to inspire its members with manliness of purpose and contempt of frivolity. A finer master of a college than the late Bishop of Peterborough never lived. A vigilant and firm disciplinarian, he was prompt in correcting the excesses of his undergraduates, exhibiting no leniency to those of them whose misconduct was all the more likely to prejudice the discipline, of the house because they were young men of superior birth, affluence, or personal style. But though properly stern to insolent offenders, he overflowed with compassionate considerateness and Christian concern for collegiate 'black sheep to whom a sentence of expulsion would have involved life-long degradation. To wean scapegraces of this unattractive sort from their vicious propensities, to restore them to physical and moral health, and to send them into the world unscarred in fame, he deemed no care excessive, no condescension derogatory to his dignity. More than two or three men, whose social usefulness equals their considerable social prosperity, gratefully attribute their success in life to the Master who conquered them with manly kindness, and reinstated them in righteous principles and self-respect, when a harsher disciplinarian would have crushed them for ever. Nor was he less abounding in sympathy for students who had no need of his forbearance and tenderness.

That his college should achieve the main purpose of its institution by swelling the ranks of the intelligent, cultivated, and zealous clergy, he was especially desirous; but none of his men—or ' boys as he used to speak of them, in his loud, hearty, shouting voice—ever started off from college on manhood's journey, by some track seldom chosen by university graduates, without words of pleasant encouragement and serviceable counsel from the shrewd and unconventional ' master.' If Dr. Jeune was still living, I should not venture thus to speak of his excellences, for which during his life he desired no man's praise, though they commanded the admiration of all who knew him. But he has departed from us; and when a rarely good man has gone to another world, the grateful commemoration of his virtues is no less beneficial than cheering to labourers who are following in his steps.

But though I have no very hostile testimony to bear against the collegiate system, which I know chiefly on its brightest side, I do not hesitate to say that its advantages were always less numerous than is generally imagined; that it was productive of inconveniences which militated seriously against the welfare of the university ; and that the university is not likely to regret hereafter the enactment which, only the other day, destroyed the educational monopoly of the colleges by permitting students to join the university without affiliating themselves to any one of the corporate houses.

Foremost amongst the inconveniences and evils distinctly referable to the old collegiate system which has been so largely modified that, so far as Oxford is concerned, it may almost be spoken of as a thing of the past,—was the exorbitant cost of university education : arising from the considerable payments exacted from the student for the maintenance of his particular academic house, and from the pecuniary extravagance which is sure to prevail more or less wherever young men, of various conditions of wealth and dignity, are brought together in familiar intercourse under circumstances that incite them to vie with one another in ostentatious profuseness and luxurious prodigality. And whilst the collegiate system must be held mainly accountable for the needless expense of Oxford culture, it must also be credited with no small share of the individual demoralization and domestic misery consequent upon the pecuniary excesses and involve-ments of collegians. Even now that they have lost the monopoly of education, the colleges will perhaps continue to be reprehensible in these respects. But the exclusive system, by which they were enabled to shut out large sections of the nation from a national seat of learning, came to an end in 1868, when the members of Convocation, giving a notable proof of the university's vigour and capability for the arduous work of self-reformation, repealed the restrictions of an ancient statute, and ' permitted persons under certain conditions to become students and members of the university without being attached to any college or hall

So long as Oxford was content to be little more than a select school for the youth of the aristocratic grades and prosperous families of English society, she declined to interfere with the monopoly of the colleges. In fairness, however, to gownsmen of a past, though not far distant time, let us also observe that, until the diffusion of education had resulted in social conditions, urgently requiring the university to enter on new and wider fields of labour, small blame attached to the conservative graduate who could not see that Oxford was bound alike by duty and self-interest to open her arms to the poor as well as to the rich, and bestir herself in the work which somehow or other has come to be very inaptly termed the education of the middle classea

No one can say that she adopted the liberal course too soon for her own interests. Throughout the last hundred years she has suffered in prestige and influence from the restrictions which made her an aristocratic academy instead of a national seminary, forbade the number of students to increase proportionately with the rapidly growing population of the country, and enriched the fortunate and idle with preferments that had better have fallen to needy and industrious students. In the middle of the last century to say that an Englishman was a scholar was almost tantamount to saying that he had studied at one or the other of the great universities. But since then the number of educated Englishmen, who never wore gown at Oxford or Cambridge, has increased so rapidly, whilst the population of the universities has stood still, or at best grown very slowly, that the non-university men of high education preponderate greatly in general society over the graduates of the old universities.

Many years have passed since Oxford and Cambridge could furnish the clerical profession with an adequate supply of candidates for holy orders. At the bar—a profession highly attractive to Oxonians and Cantabs—not half the wearers of the long robe have graduated at Oxford or Cambridge. The medical profession—which, from one point of view, and with especial respect to the character 'and attainments of its ordinary members, may almost be said to have sprung into existence, as a liberal and scientific body, in the present century—regards London as its university, and comprises comparatively few Oxford or Cambridge men. Some of our affluent merchants and tradesmen send their boys to the old universities, just as they have previously sent them to Eton and Harrow, for gentility's sake; but the educated multitudes of our intelligent, thoughtful, and powerful commercial classes acquire their learning without having recourse to either Alma Mater. The same state of things is observable in various degrees in every section of cultivated English life. Shut out in their youth from the two oldest national schools by religious restrictions or pecuniary prohibitions, the majority of considerably-educated Englishmen have no personal connection with the universities, which were once termed the two eyes of England Bearing these facts in mind, and considering also the certainty that every fresh decade will add largely to the number of our studious persons, belonging to social sections hitherto almost entirely excluded from the universities, no reader is likely to think that Oxford has been premature in opening a door, and making provisions, for a far larger population of students than has been proved to have ever resided within her bounds.

It is proverbially dangerous to play the part of a prophet, and I shrink from predicting confidently the future of Oxford. But I do not fear to say that I anticipate vast results from the recent demolition of the collegiate monopoly, and the reception of students having no connection with the colleges. Not a few of my more sedate and sternly practical friends assure me that the reform, from which I hope so much, is not the change which I imagine, and will have none of the consequences which I desire. They refuse to regard it as a measure which will sooner or later result in such an en-largement and alteration of the academic system, that Oxford will become a truly national school, whither thousands, instead of hundreds, of students will congregate from every social grade and every parish of the country,— an university where the poor student will persevere in strenuous labour under a discipline that will neither take humiliating notice of, nor give offensive prominence to, his poverty. They charge me with cherishing romantic illusions and fantastic dreams, when I ask them to think that in the course of a few generations the 'unattached students' will greatly outnumber 'the collegians;' and that whilst the latter may still consist chiefly of young men drawn from affluent houses, the former will comprise many hundreds, or even thousands, of zealous and successful scholars, content to live in humble lodgings and subsist on the scantiest and hardest fare, whilst working their way to knowledge and the happiness that springs from knowledge.

But should my anticipations concerning Oxford be justified by events, their fulfilment will involve neither diminution nor decay to the corporate houses. Sustained by their ample and steadily growing en-dowments the colleges will be no less picturesque to the observer or serviceable to education than they are now. On the contrary, instead of lacking inmates, and languishing from the effects of free-trade in learning, they will derive fresh strength and prosperity from the unprecedented populousness of the university. Redundant with students, belonging to every social class, Oxford will suffer from no dearth of rich or fairly affluent young men, whom the pleasures of collegiate association will draw to the colleges, where the mode of life will necessarily remain somewhat too costly and luxurious for poor students. Intellectual rivalry will arise between the collegians and unattached stu-dents,— but the rivalry will be of a wholesome and invigorating kind, calculated to correct the frivolous propensities of the richer scholars, and inspire men of different social classes with mutual confidence and admiration.

Is it the mere freak of imagination, and credulity, to think that Oxford may one day thus become, in the literal and largest sense of the term, a national university, frequented by the youth of the entire community, and that, when she shall have become the academy of the poor even more than of the rich, her ordinary population of students may equal the number of the scholars, whom the Amarchanian fiction represents to have studied simultaneously in her mediaeval schools ?

www.bookjungle.com *email: sales@bookjungle.com fax: 630-214-0564 mail: Book Jungle PO Box 2226 Champaign, IL 61825*

The Codes Of Hammurabi And Moses
W. W. Davies

QTY

The discovery of the Hammurabi Code is one of the greatest achievements of archaeology, and is of paramount interest, not only to the student of the Bible, but also to all those interested in ancient history...

Religion   **ISBN:** *1-59462-338-4*   **Pages:**132
MSRP $12.95

The Theory of Moral Sentiments
Adam Smith

QTY

This work from 1749. contains original theories of conscience amd moral judgment and it is the foundation for systemof morals.

Philosophy   **ISBN:** *1-59462-777-0*   **Pages:**536
MSRP $19.95

Jessica's First Prayer
Hesba Stretton

QTY

In a screened and secluded corner of one of the many railway-bridges which span the streets of London there could be seen a few years ago, from five o'clock every morning until half past eight, a tidily set-out coffee-stall, consisting of a trestle and board, upon which stood two large tin cans, with a small fire of charcoal burning under each so as to keep the coffee boiling during the early hours of the morning when the work-people were thronging into the city on their way to their daily toil...

Childrens   **ISBN:** *1-59462-373-2*   **Pages:**84
MSRP $9.95

My Life and Work
Henry Ford

QTY

Henry Ford revolutionized the world with his implementation of mass production for the Model T automobile. Gain valuable business insight into his life and work with his own auto-biography... "We have only started on our development of our country we have not as yet, with all our talk of wonderful progress, done more than scratch the surface. The progress has been wonderful enough but..."

Biographies/   **ISBN:** *1-59462-198-5*   **Pages:**300
MSRP $21.95

www.bookjungle.com *email: sales@bookjungle.com fax: 630-214-0564 mail: Book Jungle PO Box 2226 Champaign, IL 61825*

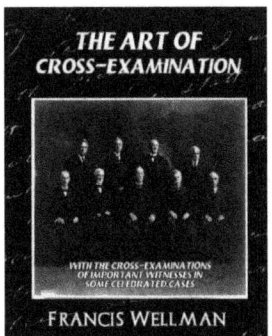

The Art of Cross-Examination
Francis Wellman

QTY

I presume it is the experience of every author, after his first book is published upon an important subject, to be almost overwhelmed with a wealth of ideas and illustrations which could readily have been included in his book, and which to his own mind, at least, seem to make a second edition inevitable. Such certainly was the case with me; and when the first edition had reached its sixth impression in five months, I rejoiced to learn that it seemed to my publishers that the book had met with a sufficiently favorable reception to justify a second and considerably enlarged edition. ..

Reference   ISBN: *1-59462-647-2*

Pages: 412
MSRP $19.95

On the Duty of Civil Disobedience
Henry David Thoreau

QTY

Thoreau wrote his famous essay, On the Duty of Civil Disobedience, as a protest against an unjust but popular war and the immoral but popular institution of slave-owning. He did more than write—he declined to pay his taxes, and was hauled off to gaol in consequence. Who can say how much this refusal of his hastened the end of the war and of slavery ?

Law   ISBN: *1-59462-747-9*

Pages: 48
MSRP $7.45

Dream Psychology Psychoanalysis for Beginners
Sigmund Freud

QTY

Sigmund Freud, born Sigismund Schlomo Freud (May 6, 1856 - September 23, 1939), was a Jewish-Austrian neurologist and psychiatrist who co-founded the psychoanalytic school of psychology. Freud is best known for his theories of the unconscious mind, especially involving the mechanism of repression; his redefinition of sexual desire as mobile and directed towards a wide variety of objects; and his therapeutic techniques, especially his understanding of transference in the therapeutic relationship and the presumed value of dreams as sources of insight into unconscious desires.

Psychology   ISBN: *1-59462-905-6*

Pages: 196
MSRP $15.45

The Miracle of Right Thought
Orison Swett Marden

QTY

Believe with all of your heart that you will do what you were made to do. When the mind has once formed the habit of holding cheerful, happy, prosperous pictures, it will not be easy to form the opposite habit. It does not matter how improbable or how far away this realization may see, or how dark the prospects may be, if we visualize them as best we can, as vividly as possible, hold tenaciously to them and vigorously struggle to attain them, they will gradually become actualized, realized in the life. But a desire, a longing without endeavor, a yearning abandoned or held indifferently will vanish without realization.

Self Help   ISBN: *1-59462-644-8*

Pages: 360
MSRP $25.45

www.bookjungle.com email: sales@bookjungle.com fax: 630-214-0564 mail: Book Jungle PO Box 2226 Champaign, IL 61825

QTY

☐	**The Rosicrucian Cosmo-Conception Mystic Christianity** by *Max Heindel*	**ISBN: *1-59462-188-8*** **$38.95**
	The Rosicrucian Cosmo-conception is not dogmatic, neither does it appeal to any other authority than the reason of the student. It is: not controversial, but is: sent forth in the, hope that it may help to clear...	*New Age/Religion Pages 646*
☐	**Abandonment To Divine Providence** by *Jean-Pierre de Caussade*	**ISBN: *1-59462-228-0*** **$25.95**
	"The Rev. Jean Pierre de Caussade was one of the most remarkable spiritual writers of the Society of Jesus in France in the 18th Century. His death took place at Toulouse in 1751. His works have gone through many editions and have been republished...	*Inspirational/Religion Pages 400*
☐	**Mental Chemistry** by *Charles Haanel*	**ISBN: *1-59462-192-6*** **$23.95**
	Mental Chemistry allows the change of material conditions by combining and appropriately utilizing the power of the mind. Much like applied chemistry creates something new and unique out of careful combinations of chemicals the mastery of mental chemistry...	*New Age Pages 354*
☐	**The Letters of Robert Browning and Elizabeth Barret Barrett 1845-1846 vol II**	**ISBN: *1-59462-193-4*** **$35.95**
	by *Robert Browning* and *Elizabeth Barrett*	*Biographies Pages 596*
☐	**Gleanings In Genesis (volume I)** by *Arthur W. Pink*	**ISBN: *1-59462-130-6*** **$27.45**
	Appropriately has Genesis been termed "the seed plot of the Bible" for in it we have, in germ form, almost all of the great doctrines which are afterwards fully developed in the books of Scripture which follow...	*Religion/Inspirational Pages 420*
☐	**The Master Key** by *L. W. de Laurence*	**ISBN: *1-59462-001-6*** **$30.95**
	In no branch of human knowledge has there been a more lively increase of the spirit of research during the past few years than in the study of Psychology, Concentration and Mental Discipline. The requests for authentic lessons in Thought Control, Mental Discipline and...	*New Age/Business Pages 422*
☐	**The Lesser Key Of Solomon Goetia** by *L. W. de Laurence*	**ISBN: *1-59462-092-X*** **$9.95**
	This translation of the first book of the "Lernegton" which is now for the first time made accessible to students of Talismanic Magic was done, after careful collation and edition, from numerous Ancient Manuscripts in Hebrew, Latin, and French...	*New Age/Occult Pages 92*
☐	**Rubaiyat Of Omar Khayyam** by *Edward Fitzgerald*	**ISBN:*1-59462-332-5*** **$13.95**
	Edward Fitzgerald, whom the world has already learned, in spite of his own efforts to remain within the shadow of anonymity, to look upon as one of the rarest poets of the century, was born at Bredfield, in Suffolk, on the 31st of March, 1809. He was the third son of John Purcell...	*Music Pages 172*
☐	**Ancient Law** by *Henry Maine*	**ISBN: *1-59462-128-4*** **$29.95**
	The chief object of the following pages is to indicate some of the earliest ideas of mankind, as they are reflected in Ancient Law, and to point out the relation of those ideas to modern thought.	*Religiom/History Pages 452*
☐	**Far-Away Stories** by *William J. Locke*	**ISBN: *1-59462-129-2*** **$19.45**
	"Good wine needs no bush, but a collection of mixed vintages does. And this book is just such a collection. Some of the stories I do not want to remain buried for ever in the museum files of dead magazine-numbers an author's not unpardonable vanity..."	*Fiction Pages 272*
☐	**Life of David Crockett** by *David Crockett*	**ISBN: *1-59462-250-7*** **$27.45**
	"Colonel David Crockett was one of the most remarkable men of the times in which he lived. Born in humble life, but gifted with a strong will, an indomitable courage, and unremitting perseverance...	*Biographies/New Age Pages 424*
☐	**Lip-Reading** by *Edward Nitchie*	**ISBN: *1-59462-206-X*** **$25.95**
	Edward B. Nitchie, founder of the New York School for the Hard of Hearing, now the Nitchie School of Lip-Reading, Inc, wrote "LIP-READING Principles and Practice". The development and perfecting of this meritorious work on lip-reading was an undertaking...	*How-to Pages 400*
☐	**A Handbook of Suggestive Therapeutics, Applied Hypnotism, Psychic Science**	**ISBN: *1-59462-214-0*** **$24.95**
	by *Henry Munro*	*Health/New Age/Health/Self-help Pages 376*
☐	**A Doll's House: and Two Other Plays** by *Henrik Ibsen*	**ISBN: *1-59462-112-8*** **$19.95**
	Henrik Ibsen created this classic when in revolutionary 1848 Rome. Introducing some striking concepts in playwriting for the realist genre, this play has been studied the world over.	*Fiction/Classics/Plays 308*
☐	**The Light of Asia** by *sir Edwin Arnold*	**ISBN: *1-59462-204-3*** **$13.95**
	In this poetic masterpiece, Edwin Arnold describes the life and teachings of Buddha. The man who was to become known as Buddha to the world was born as Prince Gautama of India but he rejected the worldly riches and abandoned the reigns of power when...	*Religion/History/Biographies Pages 170*
☐	**The Complete Works of Guy de Maupassant** by *Guy de Maupassant*	**ISBN: *1-59462-157-8*** **$16.95**
	"For days and days, nights and nights, I had dreamed of that first kiss which was to consecrate our engagement, and I knew not on what spot I should put my lips..."	*Fiction/Classics Pages 240*
☐	**The Art of Cross-Examination** by *Francis L. Wellman*	**ISBN: *1-59462-309-0*** **$26.95**
	Written by a renowned trial lawyer, Wellman imparts his experience and uses case studies to explain how to use psychology to extract desired information through questioning.	*How-to/Science/Reference Pages 408*
☐	**Answered or Unanswered?** by *Louisa Vaughan*	**ISBN: *1-59462-248-5*** **$10.95**
	Miracles of Faith in China	*Religion Pages 112*
☐	**The Edinburgh Lectures on Mental Science (1909)** by *Thomas*	**ISBN: *1-59462-008-3*** **$11.95**
	This book contains the substance of a course of lectures recently given by the writer in the Queen Street Hall, Edinburgh. Its purpose is to indicate the Natural Principles governing the relation between Mental Action and Material Conditions...	*New Age/Psychology Pages 148*
☐	**Ayesha** by *H. Rider Haggard*	**ISBN: *1-59462-301-5*** **$24.95**
	Verily and indeed it is the unexpected that happens! Probably if there was one person upon the earth from whom the Editor of this, and of a certain previous history, did not expect to hear again...	*Classics Pages 380*
☐	**Ayala's Angel** by *Anthony Trollope*	**ISBN: *1-59462-352-X*** **$29.95**
	The two girls were both pretty, but Lucy who was twenty-one who supposed to be simple and comparatively unattractive, whereas Ayala was credited, as her Bombwhat romantic name might show, with poetic charm and a taste for romance. Ayala when her father died was nineteen...	*Fiction Pages 484*
☐	**The American Commonwealth** by *James Bryce*	**ISBN: *1-59462-286-8*** **$34.45**
	An interpretation of American democratic political theory. It examines political mechanics and society from the perspective of Scotsman James Bryce	*Politics Pages 572*
☐	**Stories of the Pilgrims** by *Margaret P. Pumphrey*	**ISBN: *1-59462-116-0*** **$17.95**
	This book explores pilgrims religious oppression in England as well as their escape to Holland and eventual crossing to America on the Mayflower, and their early days in New England...	*History Pages 268*

www.bookjungle.com email: sales@bookjungle.com fax: 630-214-0564 mail: Book Jungle PO Box 2226 Champaign, IL 61825

			QTY
The Fasting Cure by *Sinclair Upton*	**ISBN:** *1-59462-222-1*	**$13.95**	☐
In the Cosmopolitan Magazine for May, 1910, and in the Contemporary Review (London) for April, 1910, I published an article dealing with my experiences in fasting. I have written a great many magazine articles, but never one which attracted so much attention...		*New Age/Self Help/Health Pages 164*	
Hebrew Astrology by *Sepharial*	**ISBN:** *1-59462-308-2*	**$13.45**	☐
In these days of advanced thinking it is a matter of common observation that we have left many of the old landmarks behind and that we are now pressing forward to greater heights and to a wider horizon than that which represented the mind-content of our progenitors...		*Astrology Pages 144*	
Thought Vibration or The Law of Attraction in the Thought World	**ISBN:** *1-59462-127-6*	**$12.95**	☐
by *William Walker Atkinson*		*Psychology/Religion Pages 144*	
Optimism by *Helen Keller*	**ISBN:** *1-59462-108-X*	**$15.95**	☐
Helen Keller was blind, deaf, and mute since 19 months old, yet famously learned how to overcome these handicaps, communicate with the world, and spread her lectures promoting optimism. An inspiring read for everyone...		*Biographies/Inspirational Pages 84*	
Sara Crewe by *Frances Burnett*	**ISBN:** *1-59462-360-0*	**$9.45**	☐
In the first place, Miss Minchin lived in London. Her home was a large, dull, tall one, in a large, dull square, where all the houses were alike, and all the sparrows were alike, and where all the door-knockers made the same heavy sound...		*Childrens/Classic Pages 88*	
The Autobiography of Benjamin Franklin by *Benjamin Franklin*	**ISBN:** *1-59462-135-7*	**$24.95**	☐
The Autobiography of Benjamin Franklin has probably been more extensively read than any other American historical work, and no other book of its kind has had such ups and downs of fortune. Franklin lived for many years in England, where he was agent...		*Biographies/History Pages 332*	

Name	
Email	
Telephone	
Address	
City, State ZIP	

☐ Credit Card   ☐ Check / Money Order

Credit Card Number	
Expiration Date	
Signature	

Please Mail to: Book Jungle
PO Box 2226
Champaign, IL 61825
or Fax to: 630-214-0564

ORDERING INFORMATION

web: *www.bookjungle.com*
email: *sales@bookjungle.com*
fax: *630-214-0564*
mail: *Book Jungle PO Box 2226 Champaign, IL 61825*
or PayPal *to sales@bookjungle.com*

Please contact us for bulk discounts

DIRECT-ORDER TERMS

**20% Discount if You Order
Two or More Books**
Free Domestic Shipping!
Accepted: Master Card, Visa,
Discover, American Express

www.ingramcontent.com/pod-product-compliance
Lightning Source LLC
Chambersburg PA
CBHW081231170426
43198CB00017B/2721